SURVIVING
SHARKS
AND OTHER DANGEROUS CREATURES

TEN TRUE TALES

SURVIVING SHARKS
AND OTHER DANGEROUS CREATURES

BY ALLAN ZULLO

SCHOLASTIC INC.

New York   Toronto   London   Auckland   Sydney
Mexico City   New Delhi   Hong Kong   Buenos Aires

ISBN 0-439-79207-X

Copyright © 2006 by The Wordsellers, Inc.

All rights reserved. Published by Scholastic Inc.

SCHOLASTIC and associated logos are trademarks and/or registered trademarks of Scholastic Inc.

12 11 10 9 8 7 6 5 4 3 2 1   6 7 8 9 10 11/0

Printed in the U.S.A.

First printing, January 2006

To Janet Shisler, whose teaching skills I admire
and whose friendship I value. —A.Z.

CONTENTS

WILD AND WOOLLY

A grizzly fishes for salmon. A cougar lounges on a boulder. An alligator trolls in a swamp. A wolf stalks its prey. In their natural habitats, wild animals are a sight to behold — from a safe distance.

But on rare occasions, they can pose a deadly threat to humans. Sometimes with little or no warning, wild animals attack.

Usually, a dangerous conflict occurs because the animal's habitat — the area in which it lives — has shrunk due to the construction of roads and houses in what was once an untouched natural environment. As a result, there are more encounters between animals and people. Few wild animals will pick a fight with humans, but most will defend themselves if cornered or surprised, and females will aggressively defend their young. Sometimes attacks happen to people who act foolishly or carelessly or who have been mistaken for natural prey. And then there are those victims who simply had the bad luck to be in the wrong place at the wrong time.

In this book you will read 10 incredible life-and-death ordeals of young people who battled ferocious wild animals, such as a merciless great white shark off the coast of California and an enraged moose in the winter woods of Maine. These stories are based on or inspired by true accounts ripped from the headlines. Although the details of the attacks are accurate, the dialogue and many scenes have been dramatized, and names and some places have been changed to protect everyone's privacy.

It's easy to fear sharks, bears, alligators, cougars, wolves, and other dangerous creatures, but there's something else you should keep in mind: The stories featured in this book are accounts of extremely rare attacks on young people.

The chances of you getting hurt while playing an everyday sport is tens of thousands of times greater than of you ever getting attacked by a wild animal. Roughly 3.5 million children ages 14 and under are treated for sports-related injuries each year. About 275,000 kids go to the emergency room every year for bicycle injuries, while another 200,000 suffer serious injuries from playground accidents.

Compare those figures to the number of people of any age in North America who are attacked in a typical year by a shark (35), bear (10), alligator (8), cougar (5), or wolf (fewer than 1). The number of people hurt by a wild animal is very tiny when stacked up against those hurt by the dog — man's best friend — whose bites cause 750,000 people to seek medical treatment every year.

Remember, all wild animals have a purpose and a right to exist in their environment, and they deserve our respect. By staying far enough away from them and by not harassing or trying to feed them, we can safely marvel at nature's awesome creatures.

—A. Z.

ATTACK OF THE GREAT WHITE

"All I could see, really, was its teeth out of the corner of my eye. It struck me so quickly I didn't have any idea what was going on. When it first hit me, it was such a hard blow. I mean, it really hit hard. Only then did I realize that this huge shark — it must have been fifteen feet — had bit me in the back and chest and was shaking my body violently. But as quickly as it began, the attack was over. The shark just let go of me and I came to the surface, and the water was turning dark all around me with blood...."

"Dude, what are you watching?"

Chad Cain jerked up from the couch, startled by the arrival of his best friend, Mick Kincaid, who had let himself into the house after he had knocked on the front door and found it unlocked.

"Man, you scared me," said Chad. "I'm watching this intense show on shark attacks. This surfer was just describing how he was attacked by a great white off the coast of California."

"Cool," said Mick as he plopped into an easy chair next to the couch.

Their eyes now glued to the wide-screen TV in the Cains' family room, the two teens whistled in awe as the attack victim showed off a crescent-shaped scar that stretched from his back to his chest. Moments later, when underwater footage showed a great white attacking an iron cage that was protecting a photographer, the show's narrator said, "They strike with no warning and little chance of escape."

Turning away from the TV, Chad asked Mick, "How many great whites have you ever seen when you're surfing or snorkeling?"

"Maybe one, but it wasn't very big. How about you?"

"I've seen as many great whites as the number of times Maria Cortez has agreed to go out with me — zero, *nada*."

"Maybe it's time you gave up on her, dude."

"I've only tried twice. I can't give up yet. She's smart and funny and pretty...."

"And she's flirting with Bud McAllister, who's smart and funny and...no offense, dude...prettier than you."

Chad grabbed a cushion off the couch and flung it at

Mick, who caught it with one hand and fired it back at his friend. "Enough about sharks and girls. Come on, Chad, put on the Lakers game."

Chad glanced back at the TV screen. A shark expert was explaining what to do in case of a shark attack: "The odds of someone drowning at a beach in the United States are one in three and a half million. The odds of being attacked by a shark are one in eleven and a half million. If a shark actually gets you in its mouth, I advise you to be aggressive. Playing dead does not work, so pound the shark in any way possible. Try to claw at the eyes and gill openings because they are two very sensitive areas. If the shark releases you, do all you can to exit the water as quickly as possible because with your blood in the water, the shark could very well return for a repeat attack...."

"Hey, dude," Mick said to Chad, "the game?"

"Huh? Oh, yeah." Chad hit the remote and switched to the Lakers game. "So what time are we going tomorrow?"

"My dad says we should leave no later than eight A.M. We'll pick you up. It looks like the ocean will be calm, so it should be a great day for fishing. I hear some boats are coming back with white sea bass and yellowtail."

The two high school sophomores, who lived a few blocks from each other, had been best friends since third grade. Tanned, lean, and sporting bleach-blond buzz cuts, they could pass for brothers, although Mick was a little shorter and chunkier. They shared a common love of the water – fishing, snorkeling, and surfing. They used to be members of a competitive swim club, but they quit because it was taking too much time away from their favorite pastimes. And now that Mick's dad had a 30-foot fishing boat, the boys spent even more time together on weekends.

After watching the Lakers fall to the Detroit Pistons, Mick got up to leave. "So, you're really not going to the party at Joel's tonight? What's up with that?"

"I can't. I have to eat dinner at my cousin's in the Valley."

"Too bad. I hear Maria will be at the party. See you tomorrow. Peace out."

The next morning, Chad woke up groggy. He had tossed and turned all night and wasn't sure why. There were no upcoming tests or term papers pressing on his mind, no big worries. *Maybe I ate too much at dinner,* he told himself. But he knew that wasn't it. For some reason, a strange uneasiness had enveloped him. He really wanted to go back to bed and start the day over again, but much later. He shuffled toward the window, hoping it would be so cloudy and windy outside that the fishing trip would be canceled. But when he opened the shade, he was blinded by the morning sun and a bright blue sky.

So why do I feel so jittery? he wondered. *Why don't I want to go fishing? I always want to go fishing. Am I coming down with something?*

Chad put on his UCLA T-shirt — in honor of the college he hoped to attend — and a pair of shorts, sports sandals, and a Los Angeles Dodgers baseball cap. He bounded down the stairs, gobbled a couple of health bars, and washed them down with a tall glass of orange juice. Then he grabbed his tackle box and two of his favorite poles, said good-bye to his parents, and walked outside just as Mick and his father arrived.

Chad threw his gear in the back of the pickup and climbed into the rear seat of the truck's three-door cab. On the way to the marina, Mick talked almost nonstop about Joel's party, but Chad's mind was elsewhere. He still had an eerie suspicion that something bad was going to happen. As Mick jabbered on, Chad was hearing only bits and pieces about the awesome band, the delicious tacos, and the major squabble between Hartley and Samantha, and…"Oh, I almost forgot. Dude, you're gonna love this. Maria Cortez asked why you weren't there."

That brought Chad out of his funk. "She did? What did you say?"

"I told her the truth – that you decided it was more important to stay home and organize your tackle box than to go to some cool party."

Chad snatched Mick's baseball cap off his head and playfully smacked him.

By the time the Kincaids' boat, the *Yeah, Baby,* was zooming toward Catalina Island 28 miles away, Chad gave no more thought to his earlier weird feelings of foreboding.

Shortly after anchoring off the island coast, the trio began catching small calicos and blue perch, using squid for bait. In the near distance, the rocky shore was teeming with a gang of barking seals. By midafternoon, the anglers had caught plenty of fish but no sea bass. "Boys," said Mr. Kincaid, "I'm going to take a little nap. Wake me in fifteen minutes and then we'll head home."

"I've had enough fishing for the day," said Chad. Taking off his sandals, shirt, and cap, he told the others, "I'm going to cool off." Then he did a backflip off the starboard side and plunged into the brisk water. Going from the sunbaked warmth on the deck of the boat into the chilly water jolted Chad's body, and he let out a loud whoop.

Mick tossed him a Boogie board to lie on. Then Mick lowered another Boogie board and jumped in.

As he lay on his stomach, Chad thought, *This turned out to be a perfect day — except for not getting any sea bass.* He had forgotten all about the uneasiness he had experienced earlier that morning.

"Hey, I think I see a turtle," shouted Mick, who was lying prone on his Boogie board. "I'm going to take a closer look." Using his arms and kicking with his legs, he was quickly out of sight on the other side of the boat, which was about 50 yards away from Chad.

Just then, Chad felt a slight change in the motion of the water below him. *It must be a passing turtle,* he thought. He looked down, but he saw nothing other than the emerald-blue sea. He didn't hear the faint, sucking rush of water beneath him, nor did he see what was hurtling from below at astonishing speed, its jaws widening.

Suddenly, a great white shark slammed into him. He felt its powerful jaws clamp down on his right thigh. The impact was so strong that Chad, the Boogie board, and the shark literally flew out of the water. He was still gripping the board when the shark flipped him over and pulled him under.

Oh, God, this can't really be happening to me! Through the gurgling white foam, Chad saw the shark's body arching above his. The shark's teeth were sinking deeper into Chad's flesh while the great white began to thrash back and forth with its human prey. The enormous pressure on Chad's leg felt like he was being gripped in a vise, full of nails. The impact had knocked the air out of Chad's lungs, and he was now struggling to reach the surface so he could breathe. *Air! Get air!* His head broke the surface and he gulped a frantic breath before he was dragged under again.

Don't panic! What did that TV show say about shark attacks? Pound on its nose. He twisted around and slammed his fist on the shark's snout once, twice, three times, but it did little good. *Hurry! Do something!* Then he saw the gills — five slits on each side, below and behind the eyes — that a shark needs to breathe. Now he remembered: *Go for the sensitive areas.* Chad reached over and grabbed one of the gills, which was the size of his hand, and yanked on it. He kept pulling on the gill in a desperate attempt to get free. Chad was running out of air. *Let go of me! For God's sake, let go!* By now, Chad's lungs felt like they were burning. He had only a few seconds left before his body would force him to open his mouth, resulting in death from drowning. But then, with no more than a second or two before the teen's lungs gave out, the shark miraculously relaxed its jaws and released him.

Chad burst to the surface again, coughing and gagging. His Boogie board had popped to the surface, too, so he swam to it and climbed on, not noticing that a chunk of the board's side had been bitten off.

Focused on survival, Chad didn't feel any severe pain because the cold water and the shock from the attack had dulled the hurt. It didn't matter, anyway. His only goal now was to get out of the water as fast as possible. Frantically, Chad started paddling toward the boat. He glanced behind him briefly and saw that his right leg was severely gashed and bleeding badly.

His eyes turned back toward the boat. *Oh, no!* A big, dark, torpedo-shaped shadow was coming toward him. It skimmed the surface, showing off its telltale gray dorsal fin. The shark, about 10 feet long and 3 feet around its girth, had set its sights on Chad. The teen stared into its large cold eyes, their black pupils centered directly on him. It didn't look curious. It looked like it knew what it wanted — Chad. And then it opened its mouth, revealing row after row of its 3,000 crooked, razor-sharp teeth — wide and serrated like a hunting knife designed to cut easily through tough flesh and bone.

The shark whooshed straight at him with the alarming speed of a freight train. Pounding in Chad's brain were the words of the narrator of the shark program: *They strike with no warning and little chance of escape.... Well, I'm not ready to die.* Chad braced himself and at the last instant turned sideways so the bottom of the Boogie board was now out of the water and took the brunt of the attack. Once again, when the shark slammed into him, the impact lifted Chad out of the water. He held on to the board, though, and when he landed on the surface, he kept stroking with his arms. *I've got to get out of the water!*

He was about 20 yards from the boat when he began yelling, "Shark! Shark!" But Mick was on the other side of the boat and couldn't hear him, and Mr. Kincaid was still asleep. "Shaaarrrk!" Chad screamed again.

Just then Mick came into view about 15 yards away. "Hey, dude, don't scare me like—" Mick stopped midsentence when he saw Chad's bloody, mangled leg. "Oh, my God!"

Mick was only a few feet away from the boat, but he started to paddle out toward Chad to help him. "No! No! Get on the boat!" Chad shouted. Without looking back, he yelled, "Do you see it?" Mick shook his head. Seconds later, Mick reached the boat and scrambled aboard.

Standing on the deck, Mick gasped. The shark's dorsal fin broke the surface and was closing fast on the plume of blood that trailed Chad. "I see him!" Mick shouted. "He's right behind you! Hurry! Paddle hard! Hurry!"

Mick reached into the cooler and pulled out several fish that they had caught earlier and flung them off the bow, hoping they would attract the shark and divert it from its main target. But the great white zeroed in on Chad. Meanwhile, Mr. Kincaid, who had been jolted awake by the boys' shouts, clutched a gaff—a long iron hook used to pull in fish—and leaned over the side, ready to strike the shark.

When Chad neared the boat, Mick shrieked, "He's right behind you! Pull in your legs!"

The shark opened its mouth and chomped on the Boogie board just as Mick and Mr. Kincaid pulled Chad into the boat. The shark spit out the board, whipped its tail, and slid under the sea.

For several seconds, no one moved or said a word. They were too stunned, their reeling brains trying hard to sort out what had happened and what needed to be done. Then Mr. Kincaid snapped into action. He poured ice on Chad's wounds and wrapped them in towels. Next, he radioed authorities of the attack and made arrangements for paramedics to meet them at the harbor in Catalina. He gunned the engine and roared toward the island.

"Hang in there, dude," Mick told Chad, who was lying on his stomach on the deck.

"I will," said Chad. "I'll get through this." Then images of the attack flooded his mind. The impact, the bite, the thrashing, the gasping for breath, the second strike, the race to the boat. And those teeth, those deadly sharp teeth. The pictures in his mind were so fresh and real that Chad began to hyperventilate (breathe hard and too rapidly) until he became dizzy. As the agonizing pain set in, his heart pounded as though he had just swum the hundred-meter freestyle in record-setting time.

When the *Yeah, Baby* reached the harbor, Chad was transferred to a waiting helicopter that flew him to the mainland, where he underwent surgery for his injuries. He required more than 200 stitches to close the wounds to his right leg and buttocks.

As he lay in his hospital bed, he recalled the eerie foreboding he had experienced earlier that morning. He started to shiver. *I knew something bad would happen to me today. My body and mind were telling me not to go fishing today. I should have listened to myself.*

He tried to get some sleep, but those horrifying images wouldn't go away. As soon as he closed his eyes that night, he saw the great white shark charging from the depths, its mouth wide open, threatening to bite him in half. Finally, the medication kicked in enough to put him into a deep slumber. But even in his sleep, he saw the shark attack again and again, like a constant loop on a video that keeps repeating the same scenes.

The next morning, a marine biologist visited Chad. After listening to the youth tell the story, the scientist said,

"In one hundred years along the West Coast from Mexico to Alaska, there have been fewer than one hundred and twenty-five confirmed unprovoked attacks by sharks on humans, and they were mostly divers and surfers."

"Oh, great," said Chad. "I'm the lucky one this year."

"Sharks don't like to eat humans. Usually, when a shark takes a bite out of a human, it lets go because it realizes it's not good food. Great whites prey primarily on rays and bottom fish. But when these sharks reach a length of 10 to 12 feet, they feed almost exclusively on pinnipeds."

"Pinnipeds?" asked Chad. "What are they?"

"Sea lions and elephant seals, the kinds you see on Catalina Island. Because elephant seals give sharks more blubber for the bite, they are the preferred target. Typically, great whites rely on stealth and camouflage, sneaking along and blending in with rocky bottoms, striking their unsuspecting prey at or near the surface. They usually take a big bite out of their victim, like a sea lion, and then wait for it to bleed to death before dining on it. The majority of attacks on humans have occurred on divers and surfers at or near the surface. I suspect the shark attack on you was a case of mistaken identity."

"But if that's true, why did it come back for another bite?"

"Occasionally, a shark becomes quite aggressive, usually out of fear."

Mick, who entered the room during the conversation, interrupted them. "Dude, I think the shark got ticked off after the first bite because you tasted so bad. It came back a second time to eat you out of spite."

"Well, I doubt that," said the scientist. "All we know for sure is that sharks are wild animals and can be unpredictable."

"Up until yesterday, I had never seen a great white in the wild before," said Chad.

"Chances are you will never see one again," said the scientist. "The safest areas for tourists are sandy bottoms, away from dense populations of pinnipeds."

For the next several days in the hospital, Chad was given pain medication and antibiotics and took physical therapy sessions. He also welcomed many visitors, most of whom arrived with colorful balloons and candy. But there was one gift that meant more to him than all the others. It was a stuffed animal — a fuzzy great white shark — that was personally delivered by Maria Cortez.

STOMPING GROUNDS

"Every day that I wake up here I think I'm in an awesome dream," Serena Garnett gushed.

Her sister, Lila, nodded. "I feel the same way. We're in the middle of Africa! Can you believe it?"

The sisters were spending two weeks in Zambia with their aunt Keisha, who was a missionary in this south-central African country. During their first week here, their aunt took them on a safari where they spotted animals that they had seen only in the zoo—black rhinoceroses, buffalo, zebras, antelope, and giraffes. They even saw a pride of lions sunning themselves near a recent kill. The girls and their aunt also canoed on a river lagoon swarming with hippopotamuses and crocodiles, and they visited the spectacular Victoria Falls.

It was an adventure the Garnett sisters would remember the rest of their lives — but an adventure that nearly turned deadly.

Serena, a freshman in a Maryland high school, was more athletic than her smaller and younger sister, a seventh-grader. While Serena was on the girls' basketball and gymnastics teams, Lila was into drama and played clarinet in the school band. Although they had never been out of the country before, they excitedly accepted — with their parents' permission — their aunt's invitation to spend part of a summer month with her in Zambia.

On this day, they rode in a pickup truck over a bumpy, dusty road toward a village that had been terrorized by elephants. During the ride, Aunt Keisha briefed the girls. "Last night, elephants broke through a fence and ate many of the crops that the farmers need to survive. The day before, a group of boys went out collecting firewood near their village and came across a party of elephants. Some say the boys threw stones at the elephants, others say they were merely watching them. Whatever the case, one of the elephants charged a twelve-year-old boy named Tiko, picked him up with its trunk, and threw him against a small tree. After the elephant moved on, the boys ran over to Tiko. He was unconscious, so they carried him back to the village.

He's awake now and has a few broken bones. I'm bringing him some medical supplies."

"I didn't know elephants would do something like that," said Serena. "I always figured they were gentle giants."

"Almost all of them are," said Aunt Keisha. "But don't forget they are the world's largest land mammals, and because they are wild animals, they can be quite terrifying and violent. Many of them have made life difficult for these African subsistence farmers — those are farmers who grow crops to feed themselves.

"Elephants need to consume huge amounts of food every day. Usually they eat from trees and bushes that grow wild, but sometimes they raid people's fruit and vegetable gardens and farmers' fields. Elephants can smash through almost any fence, and when they do, they trash the fields. They can eat an acre or more of crops that would have supplied food for a family for a whole month.

"There's also another problem. Elephants compete with farmers for water. They'll knock down walls and machinery and pumps to reach a well or borehole that the farmers use to get water. These farmers can't afford to repair or rebuild these things."

"Gee, I had no idea that elephants are so mean," said Lila.

"They're not necessarily mean," explained Aunt Keisha. "They're beautiful and magnificent animals, but they can be every bit as dangerous as lions. In fact, every year more people are killed by elephants than by lions. As wondrous as Africa's wildlife is and much as it needs to be preserved, wild animals can make life extremely difficult for the people who are trying to scratch out a living on the same patch of ground."

As the pickup neared the village, it passed barefoot women walking in single file toward their huts. They had been salvaging what they could from their trampled gardens and crops. Most were carrying hoes and gourds of drinking water; others were balancing bags of vegetables or firewood on their heads, which they had collected earlier in the day.

When the truck entered the village, children in school uniforms waved at Serena and Lila and shouted greetings in English, which is the country's official language. "Remember," Aunt Keisha told her nieces, "Zambians shake hands the first time they meet you and they always begin with 'How are you?' or 'How is the day?' Even if you are at death's door, the answer is always 'I'm fine, and how are you?' Don't ever complain. Do that much later when you know them better. And a few more things—bow to men, especially the chief, because that's what women do here. And never, ever interrupt or disagree with an older person. Got that?"

The girls nodded.

As chickens ran helter-skelter around their feet, the three of them walked to Chief Mazuba's house — a mud-walled, grass-roofed hut surrounded by a six-foot-tall fence that formed a courtyard called a *lapa*. It was within the courtyard that the family lived, cooked, and ate their meals. The chief sat on a reed mat spread out on the sandy ground under a mango tree.

After exchanging pleasantries, the chief took them to see Tiko. The boy's head was covered in a bloody rag and his right arm and leg were bound to sticks. With Serena and Lila assisting, Aunt Keisha tended to his injuries.

Lila asked Tiko, "How are you feeling?"

"I'm fine, and how are you?" he said weakly, trying to smile through the pain.

"What happened to you?" Serena asked.

"I don't remember much. I was looking at the elephant and then before I could run, it picked me up by its trunk and threw me against a tree for no reason. I remember nothing after that."

"Miss Keisha," said Chief Mazuba, "near here, the elephants have forced some people out of their villages. Many of our people have lost their food because the elephants have destroyed both the maize fields and storages in the villages.

"My own brother broke his leg running for his life after being attacked by elephants in his field. Sometimes it's dangerous for our children to walk along the road to school. We cannot shoot or harm these animals. But how are we to do nothing and let them hurt our people and ruin—"

"But most elephants are gentle and nice," Lila blurted.

The chief glared at Lila, who, after a jab in the ribs from her sister, remembered she was never to interrupt or disagree with an elder. Lila cringed and mumbled, "Sorry."

The chief frowned and, staring directly at Lila, said, "What's the worst problem you have from a wild animal in America? Perhaps a deer comes into your garden and eats your rose petals. But here, a wild animal can cost you your livelihood or even your life. Western safari tourists here love to see the elephants. They have no idea of the danger."

"What have you tried to do to keep the elephants away?" Keisha asked.

"We put up fences, but they knocked them down. We tried fire, but they got used to it. We beat drums, but they ignored them. We shot into the air, but they weren't bothered."

"There is something you haven't tried yet," said Keisha.

"What is that?"

"Chili peppers."

"Are you serious?"

"Yes, Chief Mazuba. It's being tested right now in a few other villages, and it seems to be working. It's a natural way to keep the animals away from the farms. The farmers grow chili peppers and rub chili oil and crushed chili peppers on fences. The elephants don't like it, and neither do many other animals. It's doubly good because the chili pepper keeps out wildlife, and it makes a good cash crop for the farmers. I'll make arrangements so your village can try it."

"You are a good woman, Miss Keisha," Chief Mazuba declared. Clapping his hands, he said, "You and your nieces will be our guests tonight."

"But…"

"I insist. It is a long drive back to the city. You will spend the night and leave in the morning. You must do as I say," he said, pretending to be stern. "I am the chief."

That night under a moon-kissed sky, Serena, Lila, and their aunt danced and sang with the villagers to the pounding, rhythmic beat of drums. With instructions from the chief's 14-year-old daughter, Teleya, Lila learned to play one of the traditional instruments known as a *baja,* a kazoo made out of a dry gourd. Using her athletic skills, Serena kept up with the spirited, fast-paced native dancers. Then she taught them a few American dance steps, to the amusement of the older villagers.

When it was time to go to sleep, the sisters lay on mats inside the hut of the chief and his family. Lila whispered to Serena, "I'll never forget this night as long as I live."

"It doesn't get any better than this, does it, Lila?"

Early the next morning, before the first streaks of dawn lightened the eastern sky, crowing roosters roused the sleeping village.

"Can't we sleep just a little bit longer?" Lila moaned.

Teleya gently shook them. "Good morning! How are you?"

"Fine, and how are you?" the sleepy girls mumbled in unison.

After a breakfast of tea and fresh fruit, the girls accepted Teleya's invitation to see the village's gardens and fields. While the men went off to fish, the girls joined the women, who headed to their crops, which were at the end of a 10-minute walk along a narrow, winding path through tall grass. At first light, the Garnett sisters saw the damage the elephants had caused. Half of the fields of maize, sorghum, millet, sweet reeds, and cowpeas looked like they had been crushed with a steamroller. The other half was hardly touched. The women began picking what was left of the damaged crops while the younger children looked after the babies.

When it was time for the sisters to rejoin their aunt back at the village, they said good-bye to Teleya. "Do you need me to show you the way back?" she asked.

"No, all we have to do is follow the path," Serena replied. "We'll be fine."

Five minutes later, the sisters came to a fork in the trail. "I think we should go to the left," said Serena.

Lila disagreed. "No, I'm pretty sure it's to the right."

"You've never been good with directions," countered Serena. She grabbed Lila's hand and said, "Follow me." They went to the left...and unknowingly stumbled into danger.

Because the tall grass bent over both sides of the path, the girls felt like they were going through a tunnel. They giggled until they finally broke into a clearing. Then they stopped in awe. Only 30 yards away from them an elephant cow was plucking grass. She didn't notice them because her right side was facing the girls, who were upwind of her.

"Look at that!" Lila exclaimed in a hushed voice. "Isn't she beautiful?"

"Don't make any sudden moves," Serena whispered.

"She doesn't look dangerous. She's just eating grass."

"Lila, let's turn around and walk away."

"Just a little bit longer, okay? We're not bothering her."

Seconds later, they heard a crunching sound behind them. They turned around as a young elephant emerged from the tall grass and stopped when it noticed them. "Oh, look," squealed Lila. "It's her calf. Isn't it cute?"

By now, the mother had turned and faced the girls. Seeing that humans were between her and her calf, the elephant cow became agitated. She spread her enormous ears, making her massive head appear twice as large. Then she raised her trunk and blared a warning. Serena didn't need a degree in elephant behavior to know that the mother was about to attack.

"Oh, no! Oh, no! We're in trouble!" said Serena, her voice rising in fear with every word.

Barely had the words tumbled out of her mouth when the mama elephant charged them.

"Run, Lila, run!"

Lila couldn't run directly away from the mother without running toward the calf, which now was raising its trunk and trumpeting with alarm. So Lila veered off the path and fled into the tall reeds, running blindly while hoping neither elephant would follow her. She ran into a patch of brush and skidded to a stop. "Nooo! Not another one!" An adult elephant, alerted by the others, bellowed in anger at Lila. She spun around and scampered into the grass zigzag-style like a scared rabbit. But it was no use.

The elephant chased her and, with one swat of its trunk, knocked her down. Lila rolled over, her body between the animal's two front feet. The elephant looked down at her, and Lila saw rage in its eyes. *I'm going to get squished to death!* she thought. Lila screamed. Then she tried to scramble to her feet, but once again she was swatted to the dirt by the elephant's trunk. "Serena! Help me! Helllp meeee!"

As the elephant knelt down, it rammed Lila with its head and rolled her several feet. Then it lowered itself again over Lila, who was on her back, and plunged its razor-sharp tusk deep into her right thigh like a sword.

As if it were all taking place in slow motion, Lila saw herself get stabbed, but she felt nothing. Her terror had masked the pain. *I'm going to die,* she told herself. *I hope it happens fast. I hope I don't suffer.* Rather than gore her again, the elephant grabbed her with its trunk and raised her over its head. Wiggling, kicking, and screaming, Lila tried to break free from its grasp, but her efforts were futile. Higher and higher she rose until the elephant flung her with the ease of a quarterback throwing a football. Lila flew through the air and smashed into the ground so hard she was knocked out.

About 50 yards away, Serena was also fighting for her life. When the mother elephant charged her, Serena yelled at her and flailed her arms, hoping the animal would stop. But when she realized that she wasn't going to, Serena turned and ran.

She tripped over a bush in the sand and fell face-first. *Any second it's going to trample me!* Serena flipped over to face the elephant. The elephant was already over her and lowering her head, coming in for the kill, intent on goring her in the chest. Serena screamed herself hoarse.

When the tusks were only a foot away from piercing her body, Serena grabbed them, one in each hand, and lifted herself up as though she were on the parallel bars in gymnastics class. The elephant trumpeted in fury and surprise and tried to shake her off, but Serena held on. She knew if she let go, she would be stabbed to death.

The elephant went to her knees and tried to roll her head on top of Serena, but she curled up tight and kept holding on to the lethal tusks, keeping them away from her body. But the struggle to survive was wearing her out. Lowering her head once more, the elephant tried to gore her again, but she missed and drove her tusks deep into the ground just inches from her head.

As sweat poured off her hands and her arm muscles shook from exertion, Serena began to lose her grip. *I can't hold on any longer,* she thought. Seconds later, the tusks slipped out of her grasp. *It's over. I'm going to die now.* She closed her eyes and waited for the tusks to spear her body.

But then she heard voices and shouts, so she opened her eyes. *The elephant is leaving! She's leaving!* Serena sat up and saw why. The women from the fields had come to her rescue. Wielding hoes and sticks, they were chasing off the mother elephant, her calf, and the other elephant. *I'm alive! Thank God, I'm alive!*

Teleya rushed over to Serena and asked, "Are you hurt?"

"No, I don't think so." Serena checked herself over. Other than cuts, scrapes, and bruises, she appeared remarkably uninjured. "Where's Lila? Is she all right?"

"We don't know where she is."

Serena got to her feet. "We've got to find her."

The women spread out in a line and marched into the tall reeds, calling out Lila's name.

"Lila!" shouted Serena. "Answer me! Please! Lila!"

In her frantic search for Lila, Serena kept fearing that the next step she took would be the one that revealed the crushed body of her sister. Soon Serena reached a sandy area pockmarked with brush. She was about to turn around when she noticed movement under a mound of leaves and sticks.

She walked up to it and cautiously brushed aside the

sticks and… "Lila! Oh, my God, Lila!" Serena clutched her limp, unconscious sister. "Over here!" she yelled to the others. "I found her! She's alive!"

Serena gently slapped Lila on the face. "Speak to me! Please!"

Lila blinked and coughed and looked up at Serena. "Where am I?" she asked groggily. "What happened?"

"Elephants. We were attacked by elephants."

Serena's statement spurred Lila's memory of the attack and she began to cry. And as the tears increased, so did the pain.

The women carried Lila back to the village, where her aunt applied first aid and then drove her to the emergency room in the capital city of Lusaka. Aunt Keisha and Serena spent the night with her in the hospital.

When Lila woke up the next morning, her aunt said, "You're being treated for a severe gash in your leg, loss of blood, and an infection from the wound. Lila, you're a blessed girl. The tusk missed a major artery by less than an inch. If the tusk had cut it, you would have bled to death."

"I don't feel blessed," Lila groused.

"You and your sister survived an attack by elephants. Most people don't."

"So what exactly happened?"

Serena, whose entire body ached from the ordeal, replied, "I talked to the chief and he thinks that when we got between the mama elephant and her calf, she got angry and charged at us. The third elephant heard them and came to help out."

Lila shook her head. "In all those wide-open spaces, I had to run right into an elephant."

"While you and I were getting attacked, we screamed loud enough so that the women in the fields heard us and came and chased off the elephants. If it hadn't been for them, I'd be dead."

"Me, too, because you wouldn't have found me. But I don't understand how I ended up under a bunch of twigs and leaves."

"I wondered that, too," said Aunt Keisha, "so I talked with a friend of mine who runs safaris. He told me elephants have been known to cover their own dead under foliage. And hunters claim to have seen elephants cover dead or sleeping people with a pile of branches. When you lost consciousness, Lila, the elephant probably thought you were dead and placed some sticks and leaves over you."

"So what you're saying is," Lila said with a grin, "I was in a pretty 'sticky' situation."

Serena shot back, "If I were you, I'd 'leaf' the puns alone."

THE BEAR AND THE
BLOOPER BOY

Kneeling in the fresh snow, Danny Mason bent over a pile of dried grass and struck a block of flint against a small steel bar. Sparks leaped onto the grass, igniting just enough blades to cause a curl of smoke to rise. He cupped his hands around the pile while he gently blew on it, his breath white from the morning chill. He then fed the smoldering grass with twigs and sticks until he had built a crackling fire.

Danny, whose chubby cheeks were rosy from the cold air, gently placed a pot of water directly on the fire and waited for it to boil so he could pour in a packet of Cream of Wheat for his breakfast. He had been starting his morning the same way for the past 10 days.

Danny didn't know exactly where he was, except that he was about 800 miles from home, somewhere in the remote Tongass National Forest in the lower southeastern part of Alaska. His bad attitude and grades had put him here in bear country. He was in the middle of a three-week wilderness trek with five other troubled teenagers. Two trained counselor-therapists were accompanying them, teaching them to hike, pitch a tent, build a fire, and peel back the layers of anger and sadness that had caused their lives to spiral out of control.

Sitting cross-legged on a log several yards from his tent, the heavyset 13-year-old savored the warm Cream of Wheat as it worked its way down his throat. He tugged at the red wool cap that covered his bushy blond hair and frosty ears. Mud streaked his cold-weather blue jacket, yellow rain pants, scuffed hiking boots, and backcountry backpack.

The cry of an eagle soaring above the pine trees broke the morning silence. As if on cue, the others in his group began emerging from their tents, which were spread out in a meadow, white from a light overnight spring snowfall.

It's weird, Danny thought. *I'm always the last one to wake up at home, yet out here, I'm always the first one up.*

Even though he had been out in this wilderness for 10 days, he still found it hard to believe he was here. *I don't belong with these other losers,* Danny told himself. *I've never been in trouble with the law, never done drugs, never drunk hard liquor.* But the truth was he had only himself to blame.

Danny used to be a good student who stayed out of trouble. But in middle school, he started skipping classes and then whole school days. He wouldn't finish his homework. At home, he was surly and repeatedly broke curfew. His parents tried everything they knew to get the once happy-go-lucky, well-behaved kid back on track, but nothing was working. His two younger siblings were becoming resentful of the time and energy Danny was sucking from their mom and dad. Out of desperation, Danny's parents sent him off to the wilderness trek experience.

"All right, gather around me, people!" shouted Gary Nielsen, the head counselor. When the six teenagers formed a circle around him, Gary said, "We have a twelve-mile hike today—" His announcement was interrupted by a chorus of moans and boos. "Hey, we're not even halfway through the course. Bellyaching won't do any good. We have places to go and things to see."

"What? More trees? More grass? It's all the same to me," groused Sandi Poole, one of the teens.

Sweeping his hand in an arc, Gary said, "Look around at all this grandeur. If you keep your eyes open, you never know what you'll encounter next. Maybe a bear or two, because we're definitely in their backyard. In fact, we had a visitor last night. About one hundred yards from where I'm standing, I spotted bear tracks, which I'll show you in a minute. Fortunately, the bear decided to keep on moving. And that's because we all did a great job of keeping our food secure."

They stored the food in airtight, specially designed bear-proof containers that were several yards away from their tents and suspended from tree branches out of reach of the animals. In addition to always keeping a clean camp and washing their dishes, the campers avoided cooking smelly food like bacon and smoked fish. They burned trash completely in a hot fire and packed any remaining edible garbage in airtight Baggies, knowing that food and garbage are equally attractive to bears and must be treated as if they were the same. Burying trash is a waste of time, because bears have keen noses and are great diggers.

"I want to go over a few pointers," said Gary. "If you see a bear, give it plenty of room. Some bears are more tolerant than others, but every bear has a 'personal space.' If you stray within that zone, a bear may feel threatened and react aggressively.

"Give the bear every opportunity to avoid you. If you do encounter one at close distance, remain calm. Attacks are rare. Chances are, you're not in danger.

Most bears are interested only in protecting their food, their cubs, or their personal space. If a bear doesn't feel threatened, it'll move on.

"Let the bear know you're human. Talk to the bear in a normal voice. Wave your arms. Help the bear recognize you. If a bear can't tell what you are, it may come closer or stand on its hind legs to get a better look or smell. A standing bear is usually curious, not threatening. Try to back away slowly, but if the bear follows you, stop and hold your ground. Don't run, because you can't outrun a bear. Besides, a bear instinctively will chase a fleeing animal.

"Some bears will charge, but usually it's just a bluff. They'll come within ten feet and then stop. Continue waving your arms and talking to the bear. If it gets too close, raise your voice and be more aggressive. Use your noisemakers. Each one of you has an air horn in your backpack in case you get lost and need to signal us, but you can also use it to scare off a bear." Holding up a small canister, he added, "Each of us counselors carries this little can of pepper spray that is designed to repel bears."

"What are you supposed to do if you're attacked?" asked Danny.

"If it's a black bear, fight with all your might and don't bother climbing a tree, because they are great climbers.

If it's a grizzly, which typically is brown, surrender. Fall to the ground and play dead. Lie flat on your stomach, or curl up in a ball with your hands behind your neck. Usually, a bear will break off its attack once it feels you're no longer a threat. Remain motionless for as long as possible. If you move, and the bear sees or hears you, it may return and renew its attack. In rare instances, if it continues biting you long after you assume a defensive posture, then you must fight back vigorously. But I've been doing these wilderness treks for six years, and we've never had a bear attack yet."

"There's always a first time," mumbled Sandi.

The group broke camp and headed off into the woods. Danny hoisted his 40-pound pack onto his back and filed in line. Despite being a little overweight and not in the best of shape, he managed to keep up with the others, but every day was an effort for him and he stumbled often. The trail wove out of the meadow and up a forested ridge. They hiked in silence, their footsteps making sucking sounds as they marched over the melting snow and mushy ground.

Although he didn't want to be here, Danny had to admit that the Tongass—America's largest national forest, which is about the size of New Jersey—offered spectacular scenery. The glimmering rain forest featured glaciers, mountains, waterways, and thousands of islands separated by straits and channels. But with each passing hour, Danny's backpack felt increasingly heavy and the scenery seemed less impressive.

Later that afternoon, the exhausted teens were told to set up camp in a clearing. The counselors assigned them individual spots about 15 yards apart from one another to pitch their tents. They dug a fire pit, started a big campfire, rolled several old logs close to the blaze, and ate their dinner. Then, as on the previous nights, the counselors encouraged the kids to talk about their own troubles.

As the orange glow of the flames flickered off their faces, some of the teens began opening up. The 14-year-old hated going home from school because her mother always yelled at her. The 12-year-old was depressed over the breakup of his parents' marriage. The 15-year-old who had been arrested twice for petty theft said he liked the thrill of sneaking into garages and stealing things, but always felt bad the next day.

Danny hadn't said much during past sessions. When he was invited to talk, he tried to stall and gazed toward the sky. The full moon, silver and bright, seemed to be shining directly on him like a spotlight, as though it was his turn to take center stage. Suddenly, the words spilled out of his mouth: "I've been angry a lot. I don't mean to be; I just am. Everybody is always mad at me.

A few months ago my mom grounded me for not doing my homework, so I punched my fist through the bathroom door. Another time my dad asked me what I was going to do about improving my lousy grades, and I shrugged my shoulders and walked out. He took away my CD player. So I ran off and didn't show up until the next morning. I got grounded for a month, but I kept sneaking out anyway."

"Is there something bothering you at school?" asked Stone Wyatt, the other counselor.

Danny didn't want to talk about that. But tonight he was so tired that his defenses were down. With a little prodding from the others, he opened up. "There's this guy, Pete Simpson, who's always making fun of me and has the whole school calling me 'Blooper Boy.'"

The others in the group snickered.

"Blooper Boy?" asked Stone.

"Yeah, 'cause I'm sort of clumsy, as you can tell. How many times have I fallen over a rock or a root these past few days?"

"Enough that we call you 'Tripper' behind your back," giggled Sandi.

"See what I mean? Twice I've stumbled in the cafeteria and knocked over my tray and food went flying. I fell down the bleachers during a school assembly and everyone laughed. Another time I was late for class, and as I was running, I crashed into Mrs. Williams, the principal, and papers went flying all over.

"Pete started calling me 'Blooper Boy,' and soon everyone was calling me that. I got even with him, though. I cracked a couple of eggs over the vent of his locker, and the yolk oozed inside and got on his books."

"And that solved your problem?" asked Stone.

Danny shook his head.

"Thanks for sharing, because I know that wasn't easy for you," said Gary. "But do you see a common thread in all these situations, Danny?"

"Not really."

"Think about it. Every time you get angry, it's because..."

"I screwed up?"

"Think again. What aren't you doing in these situations?"

Like a thunderbolt, the answer hit Danny. "I'm not dealing with the problem."

"Bravo! Right!" exclaimed Gary, clapping. "You don't confront the issue facing you. So what happens to you when you don't?"

"I get angry and then do something stupid."

"Danny, you're onto something." Addressing the entire group, Gary said, "When you go back in your tents tonight, I want you to think about a situation that landed you in trouble and how, if you had the chance to do it over again, you would deal with it differently."

After the session ended and the teens had turned in for the night, the counselors went around to each tent to make sure all the food and garbage had been secured. Stone stuck his head in Danny's tent and asked, "Any food in here?"

"I have some of Sandi's extra Rice-A-Roni," Danny replied. "She wasn't hungry, so I took her portion. I'm going to eat it in a few minutes."

"Okay, make sure you eat it all. Don't leave anything that will attract an animal."

Danny slipped into his sleeping bag, and turning on his side and resting his head on his elbow, he dug his spoon in the bowl of rice and took a bite. It was cold and didn't taste all that good. He put his head down and thought about what he had discovered about himself around the campfire. *I need to stop being a wuss. I need to face Mom and Dad and everyone else I have a problem with and find a way to work it out. If I can do that maybe I won't be so angry....Aw, it's too much to deal with tonight....I'm tired....So tired...*He closed his eyes and fell fast asleep. He never heard his spoon clinking in the bowl of Rice-A-Roni.

Sometime during the night, Danny began to stir because he heard a rustling sound at his feet. Thinking it was one of the counselors, he muttered, "Huh? Is it morning already?" Rubbing his eyes, he saw a figure at the entrance to his tent. "Who is it?" asked Danny, his nose twitching after getting a whiff of a fishy odor. He reached for his flashlight and turned it on.

He was seized with fright. Entering his tent with its big paws resting at the foot of his sleeping bag was a huge brown bear—a grizzly—staring right at him. Trembling, Danny gulped and told himself: *Stay cool. Slowly get out of here.* He wanted to scream and bolt, but he was afraid he would startle the bear and cause the beast to chase him.

Struggling to keep his wits about him, Danny noticed the bowl of Rice-A-Roni. *Oh, geez, that's why he's in here. He smells the food. Maybe I can distract him.* Danny shoved the bowl close to the bear and then flicked off the flashlight. He lay down and gradually wriggled his way backward out of his sleeping bag while unzipping the back opening of the tent.

Just as he squirmed free, but before he could get up off the ground, the tent collapsed, and the bear pounced on him, shoving him down. With one paw pressing on the teen's chest, the grizzly leaned closer and opened its mouth.

Danny put up his right arm to fend off the bear, but the beast chomped on his forearm and wouldn't let go.

"Aaahhh!" yelped Danny. Part of his brain was telling him, *Play dead!* But there was a stronger voice inside him screaming, *Fight for your life!*

He chose to fight. With his left hand, he punched the bear in the face over and over again. "Let go! Let go!" he shouted. Finally, after the sixth blow to the head, the grizzly released Danny's arm. The teen scrambled to his feet, but before he could run off, the bear bit him on the right side of his torso right below his ribs.

Danny fell to the ground, wincing in pain. But he wasn't about to lie still and play dead, not after he had been bitten twice. He kept kicking and socking the grizzly with all his might. As the bear growled and pawed at him, its smelly hot drool dripped on Danny, who kept moving his head back and forth trying to keep his face from getting bitten.

The repeated blows paid off, and the grizzly backed off just long enough for the teen to escape its grasp. Even though he had been told not to run from a bear, his survival instincts kicked in, and he dashed to the nearest big tree. The grizzly was right behind him. For the next terrifying minute, Danny jockeyed to the left and to the right, always keeping the tree between him and the bear.

"Help! Help!" he shouted. But because his tent was the farthest from all the others and it was the middle of the night, his cries failed to wake up anyone.

In the moonlight, he spotted his backpack on the ground next to his collapsed tent. *That's it!* he thought. *The air horn is in there. If I can just get to it —*

While he and the bear continued to dance around the tree, Danny quickly leaned down and picked up a fallen branch. He reached around the tree and jabbed the bear in the eye. The grizzly roared and backed away.

Danny then darted over to his backpack, whipped it open, and rummaged around inside for the air horn. *Hurry! Hurry! Where is it? Oh, geez, the bear is coming. It's in here somewhere.* The bear was now only a few yards away. Danny had nearly run out of time. *Got it!* He pulled out the air horn, and just as the grizzly reached him, Danny blew the horn in its face.

The blast startled the bear so much it stopped in its tracks. Slowly, Danny backpedaled, never taking his eyes off the beast. When the bear began walking toward him, Danny gave the air horn another blast, again causing the grizzly to halt. Danny wanted to flee, but he fought the urge. He was in a clearing, so there was nowhere to hide. He didn't want to run toward the other tents because that would endanger the lives of the rest of the group. A sprint into the woods where he could climb a tree didn't seem possible now that the bear was blocking his way.

Once again, the beast advanced toward Danny,

although much more warily. When the grizzly was only a few yards away from him, Danny squeezed the trigger on the air horn. But only a little squeak came out. *Oh, no! I used it all up!*

As the bear closed in for another mauling, Gary suddenly leaped in front of Danny and squirted the grizzly with pepper spray. The bear shook its head and then reared. Gary gave the beast another shot of spray, causing the grizzly to snarl and stand up again.

Still the bear refused to leave. But then Stone arrived and fired a flare at the grizzly's feet. The beast decided it wanted no more of these humans, and with one final growl, it turned around and rambled into the forest.

The two counselors rushed over to Danny, who stood almost in a trance from shock. "Are you hurt?" asked Gary.

In his struggle to survive, Danny hadn't had time to worry about his injuries. But now that the danger was over, he felt a searing pain in his right arm and the right side of his torso. When the counselors trained their flashlights on him, they saw his shirt was tattered and soaked in blood. He was becoming woozy.

The counselors carried him to Gary's tent. While they treated the wounds with a first aid kit, Danny told them what had happened.

"It was smart of you to grab the air horn," said Stone.

"Not only did that stop the bear from attacking you again, but it woke us up."

"Still, it was all my fault," Danny said. "None of this would've happened if I hadn't left the Rice-A-Roni out. I'm such a loser."

"Danny, that's not true," said Gary. "You're a winner. Why, you're the baddest guy in the woods. You just punched out a grizzly."

Danny grinned. "Yeah, I guess I did. I dealt with the situation, didn't I?"

With the help of the counselors, Danny walked a mile to a bay where an emergency medical crew arrived by floatplane at daybreak and took him to Ketchikan General Hospital. He was treated for two deep puncture wounds to his right arm and a half dozen more on his back and lower chest. Released a few hours later, Danny was sent home to heal physically and emotionally.

Meanwhile, two state troopers and two U.S. Forest Service employees arrived at the campsite and searched for the dangerous bear. They found it—a 400-pound female—and had no choice but to kill her. There were no signs she had any cubs with her.

Back home, Danny's parents apologized for sending him off to the wilderness and into harm's way. "You have nothing to be sorry for," said Danny. "I'm the one who needs to apologize to you. If I hadn't caused you all that grief, you wouldn't have had to send me away. But, you know, in a strange way, I'm kind of glad the bear attacked me. It taught me something about myself."

The next day, when Danny returned to class, he was the talk of the school because his ordeal had been front-page news in the local newspaper and the lead story on all the newscasts.

At lunch hour, his number-one nemesis, Pete Simpson, and Simpson's posse surrounded him at his locker. "What's up, Blooper Boy?" said Pete.

Danny slammed the locker and stared Pete right in the eye. "I'm going to tell you one time and one time only. Don't ever call me Blooper Boy again, understand? My name is Danny Mason—and don't you forget it!"

Pete was about to spout a wisecrack and challenge Danny when a member of the bully's posse whispered to Pete, "He fought a bear. He's not afraid of you anymore."

After Pete mulled that thought over for a moment, he broke out in a friendly grin and said, "Hey, chill, Bloo…uh, I mean…Danny." Then Pete and his pals walked away. No one ever called Danny Mason "Blooper Boy" again.

IN A TIGHT SQUEEZE

Never in her worst nightmares could Alexa Famosa have imagined anything more terrifying, more traumatic, more alarming than that heart-stopping night. For a year afterward, the mere mention of the word *python*—for that matter, the word *snake*—triggered bursts of chills so dreadful that when they would slither up her spine, her entire body would shudder.

But it was understandable.

When Alexa went to bed at night, she would swipe the covers with her legs to make sure that there wasn't a snake hiding beneath them. If she glimpsed an image of a snake in a magazine or on TV, she would scream. She would get scared just from seeing a snakeskin pattern, even if it was only on a piece of fabric and not the real thing.

She couldn't help it, not after what she had gone through.

While walking down the bustling sidewalks of New York City, she constantly would keep her eyes peeled for people strolling with pet snakes wrapped around them. On the rare times that she spotted such a person, Alexa would shriek. She would tremble in pet stores, knowing there might be snakes there even if she didn't see them.

But no one laughed at her, at least not those who knew the story of that horrifying attack.

The Burmese python is one of the world's biggest snakes. Although as a hatchling it weighs only about four ounces and measures between 18 and 24 inches, it can weigh up to 225 pounds and grow to more than 20 feet long as an adult. It lives mostly in Southeast Asia in various habitats including lush riverbanks, rain forests, grasslands, and mountains. It can be found on the ground, in the trees, and in the water.

Its favorite foods include rabbits, rodents and other small mammals, snakes, and birds. If a large python lives near a farm, it will eat chickens, pigs, and other farm animals.

A python is a constrictor, so it isn't poisonous. To find prey, it relies on its sense of smell from an organ in the roof of its mouth. When it detects a prey's scent, the python will ambush the animal and, with the snake's sharp, back-curving teeth, bite into the victim. When the animal tries to pull away, the snake's teeth dig in deeper. The python then coils itself around its prey and squeezes it until the victim suffocates. Because the snake has hinged jaws, it can open its mouth wide enough to swallow its prey whole. The python, which can live as long as 25 years, typically eats about once a week.

Eleven-year-old Alexa Famosa didn't know any of these facts. She didn't even know the difference between a python and a rat snake. She was a city girl growing up in New York and had never seen a live snake until she entered the World of Reptiles at the Bronx Zoo during her fifth-grade class field trip. She didn't find the snakes very impressive. "They just kind of lie there all curled up," she said to her best friend, Rashanda Marquis. "They don't seem like they'd be very cuddly."

"Eeww," Rashanda said with a shiver. "They give me the creeps."

"We live in a big city," said Alexa. "It's not like we're ever going to see any of them outside."

"Well, who knows? Maybe they're hiding in the grass in Central Park or maybe someone has one as a pet and it escapes...."

"Rashanda, you have a better chance of getting your own show on TV than of ever seeing a wild snake in the city."

As they walked to another glass cage that held a timber rattlesnake, Alexa devilishly hissed in Rashanda's ear and slowly ran her fingers across her friend's back. Rashanda jumped and squealed, sparking laughter among the kids nearby. "Girl, that's not funny," Rashanda said with a mock frown. "I'll get even with you, you wait and see."

The short, slender girl playfully bumped Alexa, but because Alexa was big-boned and stocky, she didn't budge. In retaliation, Alexa put her arm around Rashanda and jangled her charm bracelet. "Hear that rattling, Rashanda? Look out for the rattlesnake."

"You're cold, girl," Rashanda grumbled good-naturedly. "But you'll get yours. What goes around, comes around."

That Saturday while shopping with her mother, Rashanda dragged her into a novelty store. "Please, Mom, I've got to buy a snake."

"They sell snakes in here?"

"Only fake ones. Help me find one. I want to play a joke on Alexa."

Ten minutes later they walked out of the shop with a realistic-looking green-and-black rubber snake. "This will freak her," gloated Rashanda. "I have it all figured out. On Monday, I'm going to spread a rumor that Dante Marino brought a snake to class and that it escaped. Then, during our lunch break, I'll slip this in Alexa's desk and when she opens it, she'll scream like a scaredy-cat."

On that same Saturday, Alexa and her parents visited longtime family friends, the Javiers, in New Jersey. Alexa enjoyed seeing the Javiers because they had a beautiful three-story house — much bigger than the Famosas' apartment. Besides, the Javiers were animal lovers who had adopted two terriers and two calico cats that loved playing with Alexa.

When the Famosas arrived, the dogs jumped all over her. She took them outside, and for the next half hour played catch-and-retrieve using tennis balls. When she went back inside and sat down, two purring cats lounged on her lap.

A short while later, the Javiers' 15-year-old son, Felo, came home. After exchanging pleasantries with the Famosas, he told Alexa, "I want you to meet Chica."

"Who's that?"

"She's not a who, but a what. She's my pet. I got her a few months ago, after your last visit here. Follow me."

They walked to the basement, which had several rooms, including one where Felo kept his weight-lifting equipment — and Chica. He turned on the lights and pointed to a large glass cage that was three feet deep and extended the length of the room and halfway up the wall. Inside was a mini pond, grass, rocks, and a black-and-tan mound. When the mound moved, Alexa realized that it was really a huge snake that was beginning to uncoil.

"So what do you think of my Chica?" Felo asked.

Goose bumps prickled up and down Alexa's arms. "What is it?"

"A Burmese python. Isn't she beautiful?"

"I guess, if you're into snakes. Tell me about her."

"She's four years old and is about eight feet long and ten inches around and weighs about fifty pounds. I got her from a friend of mine, Hector Campos. He couldn't take care of Chica anymore because she was getting too big — that and the fact she escaped once and Hector's mama nearly had a heart attack. Hector knew Chica was still in the house, and his mama got so *loca* that they ended up calling a carpenter and he had to remove the entire basement ceiling. He found Chica snuggled next to a heating duct. Hector's mama said the snake had to go *pronto.* So I agreed to take her off his hands."

"And you got your parents to agree?"

"You know how much my parents love animals, Alexa, so it wasn't too hard to sell them on the idea. With the money I made in my summer job, I helped pay for this cage."

Alexa stepped closer and stared into Chica's round eyes. They seemed tender and sweet. "What do you feed her?"

"Freshly killed chicken mostly. I know some owners of pet pythons feed their snakes live animals, but Mama and Papa said *nunca*, no way. I'm cool with that."

"I hope you don't let your other pets get near her."

"We make sure the basement door stays closed so they don't get down here. Chica would go nuts if she saw any of them when she's hungry. Hey, would you like to touch her?"

"Well…I…um…"

"It's okay. She won't bite. She's gentle."

He stepped on a stool and unlatched the lid. With a mix of curiosity and a little uneasiness, Alexa got on the stool and reached in the cage. Chica's head was pointing away as Alexa lightly stroked the smooth skin farther back on the python's spine.

Suddenly, the snake wheeled around and moved quickly toward Alexa. *"Aiiieee!"* She jerked her hand out of the cage and leaped off the stool.

"Chica," Felo said to the snake, "why are you so upset?"

Just then, one of the terriers bounded into the room and, seeing the snake, began barking. "Alexa, help me get him out of here!" cried Felo.

While Felo and Alexa chased the dog, the python, getting increasingly excited by all the action, began slinking out of the cage.

Alexa scooped up the dog and scurried out of the room. When Felo turned his attention back to Chica and saw her trying to escape, he shouted, "Oh, no, you don't!" He grabbed her from behind her head and, needing more effort than he had anticipated, managed to force the snake back into the cage before she could coil herself around his arm. As he slammed the lid shut, his other terrier bounded into the room.

"Not you, too!" Felo groaned. He quickly picked up the dog and headed upstairs.

"I'm so sorry, Felo," Alexa apologized. "I never shut doors. I always forget to close them all the way. That's why the dogs were able to push open the basement door."

"We need to be extra careful," said Felo. "Chica got real excited when she saw the dogs. To her, they'd make a great meal."

After dinner, the adults played cards while Alexa and Felo watched TV. When it was time for the Famosas to leave, a wicked thunderstorm lashed the area, so the Javiers convinced them to spend the night. The hosts gave Alexa the basement bedroom and her parents the guest room on the main floor.

Staying in her shorts and T-shirt, Alexa lay on top of the covers and turned on the little TV that rested on a table by the foot of the bed. *I'll wash my hands and face during the next commercial,* she told herself. But she dozed off before the next commercial came on.

Meanwhile, Felo drifted to sleep upstairs as a tiny thought flitted across his consciousness: *I closed the latch on Chica's cage, didn't I?*

Like any Burmese python her size, Chica was strong and powerful — and always exploring ways to escape. It wasn't uncommon for Chica to shove against the lid of her cage even though it would never open. But this time, when she tried again, the unsecured latch failed to hold the snake in. Moving with surprising speed, she slinked silently out of the cage and sniffed the air. Chica detected a hint of the scent of prey, and that put her in a feeding mood. Following the scent, the python slithered down the basement hall and through the bedroom door that Alexa had left slightly ajar. It was about two A.M.

Attracted by traces of dog and cat scent on Alexa's hands, chest, and thighs, the python silently climbed up onto the bed where the slumbering girl was sprawled on top of the covers. Then the snake began curling her way over Alexa's body.

Alexa became aware of something draped across her thighs. Seconds later she sensed movement. She opened her eyes, but what she saw was so terrifying, so shocking, that her brain refused to accept it. It didn't seem possible that she was face-to-face with a deadly snake. *This is a bad dream,* she told herself. *Wake up, Alexa! Wake up!* She blinked until her eyes adjusted to the light from the TV. *Is this real?* Just inches from the girl's nose, the python flicked her tongue left and right, her eyes riveted on her human prey. She opened her mouth wide to reveal a row of sharp, backward-curving teeth.

Now it all became too frighteningly clear to Alexa. This was no bad dream. This was a real-life nightmare!

Alexa bolted up and let out one long, frantic shriek so strong that it left her throat raw. But her actions only made things worse because Chica was able to begin wrapping herself around the upper chest of the horror-stricken girl. Her arms free from the coils, Alexa grabbed the snake below her head, desperately trying to fend her off. But the python overpowered her and sank her teeth into her neck and then her head. *I'm going to die! Oh, God, I'm going to die!*

And then Chica began squeezing the life out of her. Tighter and tighter, the snake coiled itself around Alexa until she thought her ribs would crack. *I...can't...*

*breathe....*When Chica wrapped another coil around the girl's neck, Alexa knew she would be strangled to death. Her windpipe all but crushed, Alexa blurted one final, weak "Help!" before she felt herself losing consciousness. *I'm...dead.*

At that moment, her father, who had heard her scream, rushed into the room and leaped onto the bed. Clutching Chica at the base of her head, he grunted and strained as he pried the strong reptile off Alexa's neck just enough so she could at least gulp some air. He yelled for help until Felo and Mr. Javier arrived. The snake fought back, trying to bite them and refusing to release her grip on the girl. But the three used their brute strength to uncoil the python and free Alexa.

"Talk to me, Alexa!" her father pleaded. "Please, talk to me!"

"I'm...alive?" she rasped.

Her father yanked off the pillowcase and pressed it against the wounds on her head and neck to stem the bleeding. Then, holding her against his chest, he carried her upstairs and called 911. Meanwhile, Felo and his dad dragged the python back into her cage and made sure it was securely locked.

At the hospital, Alexa was treated for two cracked ribs, a damaged larynx (the air passageway from the throat to the lungs), and several puncture wounds.

The Javiers were devastated and begged forgiveness from the Famosas, who were so upset they didn't know how to respond. They were just relieved that the doctors assured them their daughter would recover physically, although they warned that emotionally, it could take much longer.

Meanwhile, police had called in a herpetologist — an expert on reptiles — to help with the investigation. He told the Famosas, "Like all pythons, Chica has poor vision and relies on smell to find prey. When the python got out, she detected the scent of the Javiers' pets on Alexa. As far as the snake was concerned, Alexa was breathing and had the odor of food on her, so she was probably food. When Chica thought she was a potential meal, the snake instinctively began to constrict in an effort to kill her without thinking that she was much too big to swallow.

"Burmese pythons are hardy, undemanding snakes, so they have a reputation as being good pet snakes for beginners. The fact is, however, they are large, powerful, dangerous animals. Despite what you hear, pythons are not suitable for beginners and should not be kept unless a person has a few years of snake-keeping experience.

"Felo had no business caring for this Burmese. Even though the snake was around humans since birth, she is still a wild animal with all her natural behaviors and instincts intact. Felo's failure to secure the cage nearly cost Alexa her life."

Alexa's friend Rashanda, who had a scheme to scare Alexa at school the following Monday, knew exactly what to do with the fake snake. Immediately after learning of the python attack, Rashanda pulled out the fake snake that she had placed in Alexa's desk and tossed it into the wastebasket. She never told Alexa about the planned joke.

The Famosas eventually forgave Felo, who felt so bad about the attack that he donated the snake to a herpetology center.

It took Alexa a year to get over the emotional trauma and her terrible fear of snakes. Even though she felt she was back to normal, she had changed in one small way: She no longer liked to wear tight-fitting clothes.

THE LONE
WOLF

Jon Stanton and his buddy Keith Thomas crouched low as they peered through the bushes.

"What's he doing?" Jon whispered.

"I think he's trying to feed it," answered Keith in a hushed voice. Standing next to him, Keith's dog, a Collie mix named Lara, began to growl and whine. "Quiet, girl."

Spreading the leaves apart in the bushes, the boys watched in fascination. Twenty-five yards away, the driver of a logging truck was sitting on the running board, holding out half a sandwich in an attempt to coax a gray wolf to come closer.

"C'mon, boy. I'm not gonna hurt ya," the trucker said in a high-pitched tone. "Here, I gotcha somethin' good to eat. C'mon, boy."

The wolf, an adult male weighing about 75 pounds, was wearing a radio collar around his neck. That meant he was a wild animal being tracked electronically by the Alaska Department of Fish and Game. The wolf crept a few cautious steps closer to the man until he was only five feet away from him.

"You can do it, boy." The trucker gently waved the sandwich in front of the animal. "It's tasty. Ham and cheese. Better than what ya been eatin' in the wild."

The wolf took another two steps toward the man and sniffed. Suddenly, he leaped forward, snatched the sandwich out of the trucker's hand, and scampered off into the woods. The man grinned and shouted, "'Atta boy!"

Behind the bushes, Jon turned to Keith and said, "Wow, did you see that? He just fed a wolf!"

"Yeah, that was pretty amazing."

Jon, nine, and Keith, ten, lived with their families in a remote logging camp in Icy Bay, Alaska, located amid towering old-growth hemlock and spruce trees in the southeastern part of the state. The camp was a tiny town of mobile homes that housed about a hundred workers—including the boys' fathers, who were veteran loggers—and their families. One section of the camp contained several small buildings, including a repair shop, a heavy equipment garage, and a small general store. In a clearing near the camp was a runway for bush pilots to deliver supplies. The camp even had a one-room log schoolhouse that educated 14 children from ages 6 to 16.

Although Jon and Keith were careful and never strayed too far from the camp, they enjoyed walking on animal trails, trying to identify the tracks of moose, wolves, bears, coyotes, and foxes. Lara was almost always by their side.

After seeing the trucker feed the wolf, the boys headed toward home. Along the way, they stopped in an immense strawberry field and, as fast as they could pick them, gobbled the berries until their bellies were full. Then Jon began plucking more berries and stuffing them in his backpack. "Maybe I can get my mom to make strawberry shortcake," he said.

Lara began to growl. "What is it, girl?" said Keith. Her ears perking up, Lara lifted her nose and growled again.

"Hey, do you hear yipping?" asked Jon.

"It sounds like wolves or coyotes. Let's check it out."

After a five-minute walk, they reached the crest of a hill and looked down at an unforgettable scene. About a quarter mile away, five wolves had trapped a cow moose. But they couldn't attack her because she was smart enough to remain standing in the middle of a stream that was too swift for the wolves to wade in.

Referring to their teacher, Keith said, "Mr. Edwards talked about this last week, remember? He said whenever a moose is chased into the water, it will stay there for hours until the wolves give up and go away."

That night at dinner, Jon told his parents about the trucker feeding the wolf.

"What?" thundered his father. "He actually fed a wild wolf?"

"Uh-huh. Isn't that cool?"

"No. It's stupid — beyond stupid. He could put everyone in danger."

"I don't understand, Dad."

"Let me explain. A wolf is a wild animal, and the reason why it hardly ever attacks a human is because it's afraid of us. But if you begin feeding it, then eventually it loses its fear of humans, and that creates a very risky situation."

"Why? Wouldn't the wolf be more friendly toward people?"

"No, son. Once the wolf learns to associate food with humans, it will continue to seek handouts from people. If it doesn't get that easy food, then it can get aggressive and attack without warning."

He added that in Alaska, it's against the law to feed a moose, bear, wolf, fox, or wolverine, or leave food or garbage in a manner that attracts these animals. Jon's father leaned across the table and asked, "Did you recognize the truck driver or the truck?"

Jon shook his head. "Not really, Dad. The truck was red like most of the others. The guy was sort of average-looking and about your age. Oh, I do remember one thing about him. He had a purple baseball cap. Why do you want to know who he is?"

"If I find him, I'm going to report him. This logging camp has a 'no tolerance' policy when it comes to feeding wild animals or leaving out trash. Any camp employee found violating the policy is given one warning, and if he's caught a second time, he's fired on the spot. The problem is that at logging camps like this one, workers come and go, and new ones don't have a clue about dealing with wild animals. If you see this guy — or anyone else — feeding a wolf, you let me know."

"Sure, Dad."

A couple of days later, Jon was walking home from school on a logging road with Rylan Matthews, one of his classmates who had moved to the camp a month earlier. A red truck loaded with freshly cut logs rumbled toward them, blew its horn, and slowed to a stop beside them.

"Hey, it's my pop!" said Rylan.

The driver, a man in his early thirties sporting a

military haircut, stepped out of the cab and hugged his son. "Did ya have a good day at school?"

Rylan nodded. "Yeah, but I got lots of homework to do."

"Well, I'm glad I gotcha here." He pulled out his billfold and handed Rylan two twenties. "I forgot ta give this money ta your mama. Will ya give it ta her?"

"Sure, Pop."

Mr. Matthews rubbed his son's head and, flashing a smile and a wink, said, "Now don't ya go spendin' that money."

"Yeah, like there's anywhere around here where I could spend it."

"I'll be back in two days." Mr. Matthews was climbing into the cab when he stopped and gazed at a gray shape peeking out of the woods by the side of the road. In barely a whisper, he told the boys, "If ya wanna see somethin' real neat, walk slowly around the cab, and git in on the passenger side."

While the boys did what they were told, the trucker took a cookie out of his lunch box and sat on the running board. Within a minute, the gray wolf—the one with the electronic collar that Jon and Keith had seen days earlier—emerged from the brush and cautiously walked toward Mr. Matthews. The wolf took the cookie in his teeth and then backed away for about 10 feet and swallowed the treat.

"How 'bout that, boys! Ain't that somethin'?"

Then the wolf approached him again. "Sorry, wolfie. I ain't got nothin' more for ya. I'm all tapped out. Now go on." The trucker reached inside and grabbed his baseball cap and waved it. The wolf took off. It was only then that Jon noticed the color of the hat. It was purple.

Jon didn't say much during the rest of the walk home. When they reached the Matthewses' tiny weather-beaten trailer, Rylan invited Jon inside. Despite its poor outside condition, the cramped inside was tidy, although the air smelled musty. They plopped on the couch and took turns playing with Jon's computer game.

Seeing an open curtain that revealed a bed in the back of the small trailer, Jon asked, "If that's for your parents, where do you sleep?"

"Right here," Rylan replied, with a slap on the couch. "My pop says now that he has a good, steady job driving a logging truck, maybe we'll get enough money to buy a real mobile home and I can have my own room."

"Listen, I have to tell you something, Rylan. Your dad is doing a bad thing feeding the wolf. It's against camp rules. He could get fired for that." Jon then explained why it was so important not to feed wild animals.

"Promise me, Jon, you won't say anything," Rylan pleaded. "Please. Pop really, really needs to keep his job."

When Jon headed home, he wrestled with himself over what to do about Mr. Matthews. Finally, Jon made a decision: *I'm not going to tell anyone about him and the wolf. I'd feel awful if I got him fired.*

The nine-year-old was small for his age, about the size of a classmate who had just turned seven. Jon looked even smaller because his desk was between two students who were big for their ages. One of them was Keith.

While completing an assignment in his math workbook in class, Jon reached down and patted Lara, who was sprawled out in the aisle between the two boys. Mr. Edwards, the teacher, let the kids bring their dogs to school, as long as the pets behaved. He loved dogs and, in fact, brought his canine companion, a malamute named Coho, to class every day. The dogs helped patrol the school yard and provided the kids with protection from wild animals.

On this day, Mr. Edwards was talking to the older students about the nearby Malaspina Glacier, a 40-mile-wide body of ice slowly descending the side of a mountain into a valley. "Glaciers carry rocks down the slope and deposit them at the edge of the melting ice," he explained. "They form stretched-out piles called moraines. The moraine patterns at Malaspina Glacier—"

Suddenly, Lara, Coho, and two other dogs in the schoolhouse rose to their feet at almost the same instant, charged the windows, and started barking wildly. The students and the teachers scrambled to the windows to see the cause of all the commotion.

To shouts of "ooh," "wow," and "cool," the kids watched a gray wolf with a radio collar around its neck stroll past the schoolhouse. Jon recognized the wolf.

"Hey," blurted Rylan, "that's the same one that my pop...ouch!"

Fearing that Rylan would get his father in trouble, Jon stomped on the boy's foot. Then Jon mouthed the words, "Shut up."

"What were you saying, Rylan?" asked Mr. Edwards.

"I, um, uh, was saying that my pop saw that same wolf a few days ago."

"This is very troubling, kids," said the teacher. "The wolf walked through this camp like he had no fear of people, like he was one of our pet dogs."

After school, Rylan went up to Jon and said, "I almost got my pop fired. I don't know what I was thinking. Thanks for shutting me up."

Jon glared at him. "I'm almost sorry I did. Rylan, when he gets back from his trip, you better tell him not to ever, ever feed that wolf again. Somebody might get hurt."

"Nothing's going to happen, Jon. That wolf is harmless."

"I'm warning you. If I find out your dad is feeding the wolf again, I'm going to tell—and he'll be looking for another job. Is that what you want?"

"No, don't say anything. I'll talk to him. Honest, I will."

A few days later, Keith found an old two-man crosscut saw rusting away in the camp's toolshed. The saw had a jagged blade about the length of a yardstick and a handle on each end.

Keith and Jon pretended they were loggers, so, with Lara tagging along, the boys took the saw and walked to the tree line not far from their trailers to cut down a few small alder trees. After selecting a 20-footer, they placed the saw against the tree parallel to the ground. While Jon pushed on his handle, Keith pulled on his, until the saw raked across the tree. Then Keith pushed and Jon pulled. It took a while, but they eventually settled into a back-and-forth rhythm. Soon, Keith yelled, "Timber!" and the alder crashed to the ground with a thud, startling Lara, who had been slumbering in a sunny spot a few yards away. After sniffing the fallen tree, she got up and trotted back to the Thomases' trailer.

"That was fun," said Jon. "Let's do it again."

While they cut into another alder, Jon caught a glimpse of a gray figure in the shadows of the woods. He stopped sawing and motioned to Keith. "You're closer than me. Can you see what's in there?"

Keith peered into the forest. Two beady eyes stared back at him from about 10 feet away. Then a face emerged. "It's the wolf that's been hanging around the camp," said Keith. "Do you think he's dangerous?"

"I doubt it. Every time we've seen him, he's seemed harmless."

Moving slowly between the trees but still keeping his distance, the wolf lowered his head and locked his gaze on the two boys as if sizing them up. His ears flattened back, the creature stepped out into the sunlight and began to snarl.

"I don't think he's acting very friendly now," said Keith, taking a few steps back. "He looks like he's ready to attack."

The wolf growled menacingly and inched closer to them. "Run!" shouted Keith. "Run!"

By the time Jon had spun on his heels, Keith had already sprinted past him. As Jon started to flee, he looked over his shoulder and saw that the wolf was only a few feet behind him in full gallop. But when Jon took his eyes off where he was running, he failed to see an exposed tree root. His foot hit it squarely, causing him to lurch forward, lose his balance, and crash to the ground.

Before Jon could get up, the wolf leaped on top of him and sank his fangs into the boy's back. Jon screamed in agony. His heart beating wildly, he flipped on his side and began flailing away at the snarling, growling beast.

But then high-pitched angry barks filled the air, and the wolf jumped off him. Wincing in pain, Jon turned around and saw Lara charge after the wolf. Flashing their fangs and yelping, the two animals tried to bite each other. Although Lara was quicker and dodged the wolf's lunges, the larger and stronger wolf drove off the dog.

Bleeding and in pain, Jon staggered to his feet, but the wolf pounced on him again, shoving him into the dirt. As the wolf's piercing teeth tore into the boy's back, Jon kept screaming. The wolf then bit into Jon's leg and began dragging him toward the edge of the woods. Digging his fingernails into the soil, Jon tried to find something, anything, to keep from being pulled into the forest.

Lara refused to give up and launched another attack against the wolf, causing him to release his grip on the boy. The animals kept circling each other, snapping and charging and backing off, neither one able to bite the other.

Hearing Keith's cry for help and Jon's screams, Mr. Matthews, who had been in his trailer at the time, rushed to the scene. He hollered at the wolf, but the animal ignored him and continued to fight Lara. So the trucker scooped up some rocks and fired them at the wolf, scoring several direct hits.

Mrs. Thomas, Keith's mother, arrived and ordered Lara to back off. She began throwing rocks at the wolf and kept the beast at bay long enough for Mr. Matthews to rush in and pick up Jon. As the trucker hurriedly carried the boy toward the Thomases' trailer, the wolf tried to follow them. But after getting pelted by a dozen more rocks hurled by Mrs. Thomas, the yelping wolf finally ran off into the woods.

Outside the Thomases' trailer, Mr. Matthews wrapped his jacket around the bloodied boy and cradled him in his lap. Both were sobbing — Jon from his wounds, the trucker from his guilt. "It's my fault," Mr. Matthews wailed. "I shoulda never have fed him. I'm so sorry, so sorry. I never thought this coulda happened."

Jon was in too much agony to care. He had been so tormented by the wolf that his mind had gone blank during the entire attack. Now, as he thought about those frightening moments, the terror he felt punched him in the stomach. He threw up.

Within an hour, Jon was flown by bush plane to the

town of Yakutat, where he was treated at the hospital for more than a dozen deep bite marks on his back, buttocks, and legs. After getting the wounds stitched, he was flown home.

"It was my first plane ride ever," he told Keith the next day. "I loved it, but I wish it could have been for a better reason."

Jon learned that Keith's father had tracked down and shot the wolf and turned the body over to state biologists for a thorough examination. A background check revealed that the 77-pound, five-year-old male wolf had been captured by the Alaska Department of Fish and Game when it was a 10-month-old pup. After the wolf had been fitted with a radio collar, he had been returned to his pack. But a year later, the wolf had left the pack and wandered out of range of the tracking device. No one knew where he had gone until he showed up at the logging camp.

A few days after the incident, while Jon was recovering at home, his father received a phone call from a state biologist. After the conversation, he told Jon, "The officials are puzzled why the wolf attacked you. They said he was healthy and had no rabies and you and Keith didn't do anything to anger him. They said a wolf attacking a human is very rare. Their only conclusion is that because someone was feeding it, the wolf lost its fear of humans. If I ever find out who it was…"

"Dad, I know who it is. But promise me you won't do anything to him."

"What? Why?"

"Because he helped save my life. It was Mr. Matthews, Rylan's dad."

"So that's why he quit."

"He did? When?"

"Today. I saw him and his family packing up their stuff this morning."

"Dad, please stop him. He told me he fed the wolf only a couple of times."

They were interrupted by a logger who knocked on the door and handed Jon's father a note. "I found it nailed to a tree by the machine shop," the logger said. "It's for Jon."

Jon took the note, which was written in pencil, and read it out loud: "'Dear Jon: I am sorry for the harm I've caused you. I had been feeding the wolf for the last six months and thought I had tamed him. I was wrong and you had to suffer for it. I hope you can find it in your heart to forgive me.' It's signed 'Bob Roundhill.'"

"Why, that no-good jerk," Jon's father hissed. "No wonder he cleared out of camp in such a hurry yesterday."

"Dad, that means Mr. Matthews isn't to blame. We've got to stop him from leaving. Please. He needs this job. And don't forget, he helped save my life."

"I'll see what I can do." His father grudgingly went over to the Matthewses' trailer and convinced the trucker to stay. From then on, the only animal that Mr. Matthews ever fed was Lara.

GATOR
BAIT

"Sasha, how are you feeling?" asked Mrs. Lewandowski when ninth-grade student Sasha Nichols walked into her English class.

Pointing to the sling that cradled her left arm, Sasha replied, "It's getting better every day. Hopefully, there won't be any more operations."

Sasha's teacher gave a sympathetic smile and said, "It's still so hard to believe. I just can't imagine what you went through."

"Maybe you'll get a better idea after you read my paper." Sasha handed Mrs. Lewandowski a stapled, 2,500-word essay for the class assignment of writing a true personal narrative. "I'm sorry it's a couple of days late, but…you know, it's been a rather strange two weeks."

"You could've taken more time before turning it in. You have a good excuse."

"It's okay. Actually, I would've handed this in earlier, but I had to go back in the hospital again for a little more surgery. Besides, it's hard to type on the keyboard with one hand."

"Sasha, I didn't expect you to finish this assignment until sometime next week."

"I know. But I wanted to write it while it was still fresh in my mind. I guess one of the good things about the attack is that it happened right before you gave this assignment. Otherwise, I'd probably have written something really lame like 'My Surprise Birthday Party at Disney World.' At least I had an interesting subject to write about. I mean, I hope you find it interesting."

"I'm sure I will, Sasha. After all, it's not every day that a student of mine gets attacked by an alligator."

At home later that evening, Mrs. Lewandowski poured a glass of iced tea, snuggled on the couch, and faced the English-class papers that she had piled on the coffee table. She thumbed through the stack until she found Sasha's essay and pulled it out. *I must read hers first,* the teacher told herself.

SEE YA LATER, ALLIGATOR
by Sasha Nichols

I thought I was going to die.

A huge alligator had grabbed my left arm and was dragging me underwater. I was beyond terrified. All I could think was, *I hope he doesn't eat all of me. I hope he leaves enough of me to bury.*

I never gave much thought to getting attacked by an alligator. I've lived next to Lake Concord for seven years and although I've seen gators from time to time, they were always small. I know here in Florida gators sometimes bite people and come out of lakes and canals and eat pet dogs and cats, but that's never happened at my lake. My friends and I have gone swimming in there for years without any problem.

I guess I should have been more concerned. About a week before I was attacked, my older sister's boyfriend, Mark Heller, had a scary moment with a gator. Actually, it was his dog, Homer, who had the scary moment.

Homer is a German shepherd mix, and he and Mark were walking along the edge of Lake

Monroe, which is about a mile from where I live and is connected to Lake Concord by a canal. While they were walking, Homer took off after a bunch of ducks floating nearby.

Mark called him to come back, but Homer didn't respond, which was unusual for him. Mark went over to the water and heard Homer whining. The dog wasn't moving and it looked like he was just stuck in the mud. Mark went down into the mud to pull him out when all of a sudden he realized that an alligator had a hold of Homer's front leg.

The gator let go of the dog for only a second and then got Homer's head in its jaws and started to drag him deeper into the water. Mark is a big guy and he loves his dog very much because he got Homer as a gift from his father only a few months before Mr. Heller died from a heart attack. Homer means an awful lot to Mark and he didn't want his dog to die, so Mark jumped into the water, which was up to his knees, and he began beating on the gator.

The alligator kept swishing its tail and then took Homer under the water. Mark thought he had lost his dog for good but then the gator came up to the surface close to the bank. Mark pounded on the gator's nose real hard and finally the gator opened its mouth and Mark was able to pull Homer away and get him back on land. The gator looked like it was thinking about coming out, but instead turned and sank under the water and disappeared.

Poor Homer was hurt pretty badly. His leg had been cut all the way to the bone and he also needed more than 20 stitches just on his head. The vet told Mark that an alligator usually grabs its victim by the head, like it did with Homer, and drags the animal under the water to drown it. The gator takes the dead body to a hiding place to let the flesh decay a little before eating it. That's pretty gross.

Homer's leg is all bandaged up. His head has all these puncture wounds that form the shape of the gator's mouth. It's a good thing that Homer is a pretty big dog and was strong enough to survive the attack. It's probably a better thing that Mark is big and strong and courageous, or Homer definitely would've been dinner for the gator.

You would think that after learning about what happened to Homer I would have been very scared to swim in Lake Concord. Well, the truth is that I didn't really give it much thought. I wasn't worried about gators in my lake for several reasons. First, Homer was attacked in Lake Monroe, a mile away from my home. Second, no person or pet had ever been attacked by a gator in Lake Concord. Third, alligator attacks are very rare. According to the Florida Fish and Game Commission, during the last 50 years there have been only about 200 alligator attacks on humans in this state and only 12 people have been killed. The odds of being bitten by a gator are very, very small.

A week after Homer was attacked, my best friend, Allison Kristoff, came over to my house and so did our friends Derek Ford and Austin Peterson. At about five o'clock in the afternoon, we decided to cool off in the lake because it was really hot. We each took a Boogie board with us and went in the water and floated on them.

The boys were horsing around, trying to dunk each other, and then they swam underwater and came up right underneath us and knocked us off our Boogie boards.

I got back on my Boogie board and was floating away from the others. I was on my stomach with my arms dangling in the water when all of a sudden I felt something grab my left forearm really hard. At first I thought it was

Derek goofing around. My head was turned the other way and I said, "Derek, stop that. You're hurting me."

Then I turned around and I realized it wasn't him. I freaked out. A huge alligator had my arm in its jaws! Before I could scream or yell for help, the gator immediately pulled me off my Boogie board and dragged me underwater. It happened so fast that I was barely able to get a breath before I went under.

Everything that happened next seemed like it was in slow motion and lasted a long time, but really it was probably only half a minute. I remember every detail and it still gives me the willies whenever I think about it.

The gator's jaws clamped down even harder on my arm and then it started giving me the death spin. When an alligator has a large prey in its mouth, and it can't eat it all at once, the gator rolls over and over real fast, hoping to break it apart. That's what it was trying to do to me. The alligator wanted to break me apart.

It kept twirling and spinning and jerking me, and then I heard something crack. It was my arm. The gator broke it but I was trying to survive, so I really didn't feel any pain at that time. I was running out of air and the gator wouldn't let go of me. I thought, *This is going to be it. I'm going to drown.*

Luckily, it stopped doing the death spin and I managed to get my head above the surface and I took a couple of deep breaths before it pulled me back down. When I got some air into my lungs, I told myself, *I'm too young to die,* and I felt a real strong surge of energy to fight back with everything I had. I knew the only way I could survive was to get my arm free. My biggest worry was that the gator would bite it off and I would bleed to death.

When the gator brought me back up to the surface, I took another big breath and then I tried to pry open its mouth with my right hand. I could feel the pressure of its jaws give way just a little. It was enough to get my fingers into its mouth, but then I cut my hand on its teeth. I got big gashes on my thumb and on the palm of my hand.

I remember looking into the alligator's eyes. They really scared me because they looked like a murderer's eyes. They were cold and mean.

I started screaming for help. I looked beyond the alligator and I saw both boys swimming fast for the bank. My friend Allison, though, didn't swim away. She started coming toward me. When I saw that, I thought maybe she could save me. At the time I didn't think about the danger she was putting herself in. I was only concerned with trying to live.

Just knowing that Allison was nearby gave me a big boost. I had another burst of energy and even though my hand was bleeding from the gator's teeth, I managed to open its mouth just enough to get my arm out. It was all sliced up. When I saw that, I really started feeling the pain.

I tried to lift my arm, but I couldn't. I was pretty sure the gator had broken it because I heard my arm crack when the gator bit down. I figured that only a few pieces of muscle or tendons were all that was holding it together and I was afraid that I'd lose my arm for good. I began crying, "I've lost my arm! I've lost my arm!"

The gator went under the water and I tried to swim but I was exhausted and I hurt an awful lot. Luckily for me, Allison arrived and she had brought my Boogie board. I'll never forget what she told me. She said, "I'm not going to let you die. I promise." I got on it and then she began pulling me toward the bank.

She was so brave because the alligator came to the surface again and followed us. Allison kept telling me to stay calm and that we would make it out of there. I kept looking over my shoulder and watching the gator. All I could see were its eyes staring at me and its big tail swishing back and forth. Every time I looked back, the alligator seemed to be gaining on us.

While Allison pulled on the Boogie board, I was kicking as hard as I could. I wanted to get out of the lake so fast. I wished a helicopter would come down and pull me out of the water, but of course that wasn't going to happen. I was afraid that the gator was going to attack me again. It seemed like it was taking forever to reach land but Allison kept talking to me, saying that we would make it.

The last time I looked back, the gator was gone and then I got real scared because I thought it could be right below me, ready to grab me in its jaws again. Then I thought maybe it would go after Allison. I began crying again.

We were getting close to the bank and I saw the boys with my mom. I found out later that when Derek and Austin saw me get attacked by the gator, they got out of the water and ran to tell Mom, who called 911. I could see that

Mom was crying and had her hands on her face and that made me cry all the more.

The three of them came down to the water and rushed in up to their waists and pulled Allison and me out. I sobbed and sobbed, but this time it wasn't out of fear but out of relief. Mom wanted to hug me but she was afraid she'd hurt me. She kept repeating, "Thank God you're alive! Thank God you're alive!" She wrapped my bloody arm and hand in towels, and I heard the sirens in the distance getting louder.

Allison sat down next to me and said, "See, I told you we'd make it." I never felt so thankful in all my life. I wanted to tell her how grateful I was but all I could say was something real lame, like, "Thank you. You're my angel."

I looked out on the lake and saw the gator just moseying about while three empty Boogie boards floated near it. I shuddered. It looked even bigger than I thought. That alligator had to be at least 10 feet long.

When the ambulance came, I asked Allison and Mom to go with me to the hospital. I needed them by my side.

At the hospital, I received real good care. I needed some blood transfusions because I had lost a lot of blood. Dr. John Chesterfield operated on my arm. He said the snap I heard during the attack was actually the alligator breaking the lower part of my upper arm bone when it was spinning me. I had several deep cuts on my forearm from where the gator had bitten me. The biggest gash was about seven inches long and very deep. It was nearly down to the bone, but luckily the gator's teeth just missed cutting one of my major nerves that helps control my left hand.

Dr. Chesterfield said the biggest concern was the risk of infection, because of the bacterial contamination that was in the lake and in the alligator's mouth. I've had surgery twice so the doctor could go in there and clean out everything again. He said I would have to wear a cast for at least a month and keep my arm in a sling. My right hand was cut up pretty badly but there was no permanent damage, and the bandages had to stay on for a week.

I spent three days in the hospital. Allison came to visit me every day. We have been best friends for more than two years, and now she's more than my best friend. She's my hero. It's like we have a bond now. I don't think I'd be here today without her. Allison saved my life, and

I am forever grateful for that. I was really blessed to have her there, because I think if she hadn't come to my rescue, I would have drowned, or the gator would have come back and killed me.

Allison told me later that when she saw me getting attacked, she first thought about getting out of the water to save her own life. But that thought lasted for only a split second. She said she had to be there for me because she didn't want to see me die. She put it all in God's hands. Allison stayed near me during the attack so that when I got free from the alligator, she could rush over and get me on the Boogie board and push me away from the gator. She admitted that even though she was telling me to be calm and that everything would be all right, she was really scared that the gator would come back and attack both of us. When you're scared but you do something anyway, that's real courage.

Mom still can't believe I'm alive. She said that she's never heard of anyone being pulled under by an alligator doing the death spin who lived to tell the tale. Well, now she has heard of one.

When I came home, all my friends were waiting for me with balloons and a cake and lots of flowers. I felt happy that they cared but I also felt a little embarrassed over all the fuss.

Someone asked me if I hate the alligator. The truth is that I don't. The gator was just doing what gators do. They are killing machines. They can't be tamed or act nice because even though they are big and powerful, they have a brain the size of a grape. All they know how to do is lie in the sun and eat whatever they can. They don't know any better. I guess that gator thought I was food.

The day after the attack, a wildlife officer killed the alligator. When they hauled the gator out of the water and measured it, it was 11 feet long and weighed about 400 pounds. That alligator was a big one! I never thought a gator that big would be in Lake Concord. It's not like I didn't have a warning that there could be a dangerous gator in there. I should have been more careful.

Someone asked me if I would ever go back in the water again. I don't think that's going to happen anytime soon. In fact, it might never happen. I've learned my lesson. I think that the next time I get the urge to go swimming, I will jump in a pool.

When Mrs. Lewandowski finished reading the paper, she took a big gulp of iced tea, picked up her red pen, and wrote *A* on the title page. Then she thought a moment and determined that it wasn't the right grade. So she changed it — to *A+*.

BULL FRIGHT

Ellie Lang ran through the shadowy, narrow rows of towering cornstalks until her leg muscles felt like they were on fire. She was trying to stifle her giggles because in this intense game of hide-and-seek with her cousins, the pint-sized 10-year-old didn't want to be caught.

She hoped to prove that a city girl like her — a girl who lived in a Chicago apartment, no less — could thrive just fine out here on her grandparents' 200-acre farm in central Illinois. Ellie definitely didn't want to appear "citified" to her country cousins, Katy Lang, 12, and Katy's brother, Greg, 11, who lived on the farm with their parents and paternal grandparents, Clay and Melanie Lang.

It was Ellie's first day of a two-week stay on the farm while her parents were on a Caribbean cruise. The perky curly-haired brunette was getting reacquainted with her cousins by playing hide-and-seek in the cornfield. She felt proud of herself because when she was "it," she needed only three minutes to find Greg, who had been hiding between two giant cornstalks about six rows away from her.

When it was his turn to find the girls, Ellie and Katy ran in different directions. Ellie scampered blindly down one row and then cut across five rows as the fresh green stalks slapped her in the face and made a *whap-whap-whap* sound against her ears.

She stopped and crouched in the dirt, giggling softly between heavy breaths. She was smaller than her bigger and beefier cousins and figured she would be harder to spot. Five minutes went by and then 10. She heard nothing. *Where are they?* she wondered. "Hello? Hello? Are you out there?" she shouted. There was no response.

I get it, she thought. *They probably left me here in the cornfield on purpose and went back to the farmhouse for some lemonade. I'll just find my own way out.* But in all the running up and down the rows and slicing across them, she had lost her bearings. The stalks were so plump with ripening corn that they had nearly swallowed up the spaces between them, turning the cornfield into a dark green maze. *I'll just try to follow a row. It'll either lead me to the far end of the cornfield or closer to the house.* Sticking her arms out to form a plow, she tried to walk in a straight line. *Don't get scared,* she told herself. Sweat rolled down her back and legs, and it wasn't all from the steamy July afternoon. On and on she walked. *How much farther?*

Two dozen steps later, she emerged from the cornfield, the sun briefly hurting her eyes. *Finally!* But her happiness was dampened when she realized that she had reached a barbed-wire fence that bordered the cow pasture. *Darn it. I must be at the far end. Now I have to go back the other way.* She walked along the fence line until she came to a metal gate. She climbed on it and tried to balance on the top bar, hoping to get a view over the cornstalks, but she wasn't tall enough.

Then she noticed an apple tree in the pasture about 20 yards away. She hopped off the gate and walked to the tree. She had just reached it when—"Ouch!"—a green apple fell off a branch and conked her on the head. She didn't know whether to laugh or cry. She did neither. She bit into the apple. *Mmm. Good.* She sat down, leaned against the tree, and munched on the fruit.

I wonder if Grandma and Gramps are worried about me or if they'll be mad at me. Her thoughts were interrupted by a loud snort behind her. She turned around and gasped. No more than five feet away stood a bull that was glaring at her. Its head began swaying, making its hooked, pointed horns look like curved, sharp knives dancing menacingly in the air.

Ellie's first instinct was to sprint toward the fence, but she figured the bull would run her down. So she slowly stood up, reached over her head, and grabbed a branch. Then she swung her slender body up and climbed into the apple tree. The bull snorted, moved forward, and then lay down right below her.

Now what? I can't stay here all day. "Go away!" she ordered. "Get out of here!" She plucked a couple of apples and flung them down at the bull. Other than a grunt, he ignored her. *He's huge. Like a car. And he smells bad. Pee-eew!*

Ellie climbed higher, knowing that if she fell, she would land directly on the bull's back. She soon reached a height that let her see beyond the tops of the cornstalks. The farmhouse was far away, on the other side of the cornfield. She looked down as the tail of the slumbering beast swatted a swarm of flies. *There's nothing I can do but wait him out. But what if he stays there all day? Then what? Oh, brother. My first day on the farm, and this happens to me.*

She had never seen a bull up close before. But she had seen enough shows on television to know how ferocious one could be. As she sat in a fork of the tree, chomping on another apple, Ellie thought about the wild experience Crazy Uncle Steve once had with bulls. Although he was a commercial airline pilot who flew all over the world, the family jokingly called him Crazy Uncle Steve because of his hunger for dangerous adventures like hang gliding off a cliff, feeding sharks while scuba diving, and iceboat racing. When he would entertain the family with stories of his extreme feats, relatives would tell him, "Steve, you're crazy." But the family was always fascinated — especially Ellie. She, too, had a hunger to try new things, although not necessarily as risky. In fact, it was because of her desire for new experiences that she convinced her parents to let her spend two weeks on her grandparents' farm. "I want to see what it's like to be a farm girl," she told them. Crazy Uncle Steve, who happened to be in Chicago at the time she announced her wish, thought it was a terrific idea.

During his visit, he told Ellie about the unforgettable time when he ran with the bulls in Pamplona, Spain. "Every year, hundreds of men and women run with about a dozen bulls through the narrow cobblestone streets for three-quarters of a mile," he explained. "A lot of runners get knocked down, gored, or trampled, and about every five years someone gets killed. I know it's crazy, but I had to try it.

"I was having a good run when a bull came up behind

me and bumped me in the back because he wanted to go faster, and the people in front of me were too slow. His horns were brushing under both of my armpits. I had no place to go because there was another bull on my left and runners on my right.

"So the bull threw me with his nose, and I landed face-first against the curb. I always tell people that if you get knocked down by a bull, don't move. Many people get gored and even killed when they fall and jump back up because that attracts the bull's attention.

"Well, when I fell, I smashed my mouth and knocked out my tooth. So what did I do? I got up on my knees and shouted, 'My tooth!' The bull had stopped, and the first movement he saw was this jerk sitting up holding his tooth. *Wham!* He gored me." When Crazy Uncle Steve reached this part of the story, he took off his shirt and showed Ellie a six-inch J-shaped scar on his back just above his waist. "Some bystanders pulled me away from the bull and got me medical help. I was stitched up and darned if I didn't race again the next day."

"Why, Uncle Steve?"

"Because I always finish what I start. I couldn't go through life knowing that I quit a race because of a big dumb beast. I was scared that second day, but I ran the course without a problem. I don't plan on ever doing it again, but at least I can say I did it. That's what life is all about. Doing new things, all sorts of new things."

"Uncle Steve, you're crazy!" But deep down, Ellie hoped that someday she would have the guts to be as crazy as he was.

Now here she was stuck in an apple tree with a sleeping bull directly below her. *I wonder what Crazy Uncle Steve would think about this,* she thought. An hour had passed and the bull showed no signs of moving. Ellie was getting a stomachache from fretting over her situation — and from eating too many green apples. *When am I ever going to get down from here?*

Soon she heard a *chug-a-chug.* Off to her left, along the fence line, were Katy and Greg on either side of Gramps, who was driving a green tractor. Every minute or so, Gramps would shut off the engine and the three of them would yell, "Ellie! Ellie!"

When they got closer and stopped, Ellie shouted, "Over here! Over here!"

"Where?" Gramps asked. "I hear you but I can't see you!"

"I'm up in the apple tree!"

From the other side of the barbed-wire fence, Gramps took off his smudged straw hat, wiped sweat off his bald head, and smiled. "Looks like you got yourself in quite a pickle, girlie. How long are you planning on staying up there?"

"Oh, Gramps, please help me. This bull won't leave."

"Did you ask real nice? Brutus doesn't take kindly to people who are rude."

"I told him to go away but he wouldn't."

"That's because you didn't sweet-talk him. Stay put and I'll be back in about ten minutes." He turned to Katy and Greg and said, "You keep an eye on Ellie — and don't you dare go on the other side of the fence, understand?" The kids nodded.

Gramps left and returned on the tractor, pulling a wagon with a bag of feed. He drove about 50 yards farther down the fence line and whistled to the bull. Gramps poured a small pile of feed over the barbed wire and into the pasture. The bull strolled over to him and began eating.

Gramps shouted to Ellie, "All right, come on down and then walk — don't run — to Katy and Greg while Brutus is busy eating!"

Ellie lowered herself to the ground, walked as fast as she could, and quickly climbed over the gate to safety.

"I can't wait to hear how you ended up in an apple tree," Katy said, grinning.

After Ellie explained what had happened, her cousins and Gramps burst out laughing. Ellie wanted to cry from embarrassment but she didn't dare, not in front of them.

"If you had let Brutus chase you, you could have been like Crazy Uncle Steve," said Greg.

"Brutus didn't mean you any harm," said Gramps. "Oh, he can be ornery from time to time. Like any bull, he can be temperamental and unpredictable, but basically he's a good bull."

"Except he doesn't like city girls," said Greg with a wink.

"We've raised him since he was a calf," Katy told Ellie. "About three years ago, I was out in the pasture with Gramps, and we saw that a baby bull had been abandoned by his mother. The poor thing got up and followed us all the way home like a puppy dog for about half a mile. We took care of him until he could make it on his own."

That evening at dinner, which was served on the porch on a table handmade by Ellie's great-grandfather, lots of belly laughs came with the dinner, which started with grace. While Grandma was giving her usual long-winded blessing, Gramps kept making funny faces until Ellie could no longer hush up her giggles. Grandma was not amused. After flashing an angry frown at Ellie, Grandma scolded Gramps. "Clay Lang, you stop that right now!"

"You mean *this*?" he said, scrunching his leathery face into another silly pose. The kids broke into guffaws — and so did Grandma.

Dinner consisted of food produced right on the farm, including some that Ellie had never tasted before — fresh turnips; cucumbers and onions in a vinegar brine; beets; and creamed new potatoes and peas. It also featured fried chicken, corn on the cob, and fresh-baked bread. Ellie would have eaten more, except her stomach was still grumbling from all the green apples she had consumed earlier.

"Uh-oh!" Gramps moaned. "My gums! My gums are bleeding!" He winced and spread his lips.

Seeing what she thought was blood dripping from his teeth, Ellie screamed. She was puzzled when Katy and Greg roared with laughter.

"Clay!" bellowed Grandma. "You stop that right now! You're scaring the girl half to death!" But even Grandma found it hard not to resist a chuckle.

When the laughter stopped, Katy explained, "Gramps was just fooling you, Ellie. The blood you saw was really juice from a beet that he was chewing." Turning to Gramps, Katy said, "You got Ellie good with that one."

Ellie rolled her eyes and thought, *And this is only my first day on the farm.*

The next 12 days flew by for Ellie, who did things she

had never done before. She pitched in with the chores in the morning and played in the afternoon with her cousins. She gathered eggs in the henhouse (and got her hand pecked more than once), weeded the bean field (and got her arms sunburned), slopped the hogs (and fell into a mud puddle), shucked the corn, and shelled the beans. For fun, she and her cousins built tunnels with bales in the hayloft, fished for bluegill in the pond, and explored the farmhouse attic. One thing they didn't do anymore was play hide-and-seek in the cornfield.

It all went by so fast for Ellie, and when she woke up on her last full day on the farm, she told Gramps, "I wish I could stay longer. It's been so much fun."

But the fun was about to change.

Later that morning, Ellie and her cousins were snooping around in an old, rickety, unused toolshed next to the barn. The shed still held some handmade tools that their great-grandfather had crafted in the late 1800s.

Outside near the barn, Gramps was herding the cows to a different pasture along a path that went by the old toolshed. Unexpectedly, Brutus charged toward a cow that was walking next to Gramps. With a broomstick that he often carried, Gramps smacked the bull on the head.

Brutus snorted and moved away but returned, the hair on his back bristling, so Gramps struck him again. Normally, that was all it took for the bull to stop misbehaving. But this time, Brutus bellowed and turned on Gramps. With his head, the animal drove Gramps to the ground and tried to gore him, but missed.

Hearing the commotion, the kids ran outside. "Gramps! Oh, Gramps!" Ellie shrieked.

Rolling on the ground and trying to dodge the bull's hooves and horns, Gramps yelled, "Get back inside!" Just then the bull stomped on the farmer's left arm, causing Gramps to scream in pain. A hoof whacked him in the head, briefly knocking him out.

Katy rushed into the toolshed and returned with an antique wooden pitchfork. "Go inside!" she ordered the others. Greg ran for the shed, but Ellie tripped and fell. As Ellie scrambled to her feet, the enraged bull galloped past Katy. He lowered his head, charged into Ellie, and tossed her in the air. She tumbled head over heels for 15 feet and landed hard, which knocked the wind out of her.

Ellie tried to get up, but the bull butted her, rolled her onto her back, and ran right over her. When he planted his left foot squarely on her upper chest, Ellie was certain that he would crush her heart and lungs. But

Brutus wasn't able to put his full weight on her because at that moment Katy jabbed him with the pitchfork.

The bull turned away from Ellie and squared off with Katy. *I've got to get to the shed,* thought Ellie. Gasping for breath and wincing in pain, Ellie began crawling slowly toward the shed 10 feet away. Suddenly, the door swung open and Greg leaped out, grabbed Ellie, and pulled her inside.

Meanwhile, Katy was bravely poking at Brutus with the pitchfork. He moved a few steps back, lowered his head, hunched his shoulders, and then pawed the ground.

Uh-oh, he's going to charge me, she thought. *Get away from him!*

Katy dropped the pitchfork and made a mad dash for the toolshed, the bull only a few feet behind her. Greg swung open the door, and as Katy scurried in, he slammed it shut. She and Greg then threw their weight against the door as Brutus crashed into it with his head, cracking several wood slats. But the door held.

Snorting and bellowing angrily, the bull ran to the side of the shed and, with his horns, shattered the window and sent splinters from the window frame flying toward Ellie, who was curled up on the floor, waiting for this nightmare to end. Then he began butting the opening, making it bigger with each thrust.

"He's going to break through the wall and kill us!" Greg cried.

"No, he's not!" declared Katy.

She ran out of the shed and around to the side and yelled at the bull, "Hey, Brutus, over here!" When the bull saw her, she raced back inside and shut the door and braced herself just as the bull plunged his horns through it, missing Katy's head by only inches. The bull snarled because he was stuck, but it took only a few seconds to free his horns from the door.

Katy and Greg shoved a workbench against the door. They dug in their heels and leaned on it while Brutus kept butting the door until he forced it open just enough to shove his head inside.

Despite the pain, Ellie crawled over to a shovel and pushed it over to Katy. Clutching the shovel, Katy repeatedly whacked the bull's head while she and Greg strained to keep the door from opening any wider.

"We can't hold out much longer!" Katy shouted. "Ellie, can you walk at all?"

"I—I think so."

"Okay, go out through the broken window now! We'll keep Brutus out for another few seconds! Go! Go!"

As pain tore through her chest, Ellie lurched out the window and wobbled away from the shed until she was safely on the other side of the barn. Just seconds after

Ellie escaped, Brutus busted the door and charged inside past Katy and Greg, who slipped around the open doorway and fled.

Furious and out of control, the bull butted and smashed the walls until the entire shed collapsed. Then he roared out from under the rubble, ran out about 10 yards, stopped, and looked for someone to attack.

Fortunately, Katy and Greg had already helped Gramps, who had regained consciousness, to his feet and got him over the fence to a spot where Grandma was tending to Ellie. Grandma then loaded everyone into the pickup truck and zoomed off to the hospital.

Ellie was treated for two fractured ribs and a broken sternum — the long flat bone in front of the chest that connects the ribs.

When the family visited Ellie in her hospital room the next morning, Grandma asked, "How are you feeling, dear?"

"It hurts to breathe, and I'm very sore."

Gramps, who had a cast on his broken arm and a bandage around his head, said, "Well, girlie, this is a fine way to extend your stay here on the farm."

"I told you I didn't want to leave," said Ellie. "So, Gramps, what are you going to do with Brutus?"

"Well, had you asked me that yesterday, I would've told you I plan to turn him into a bunch of steaks. But

I think I'll donate him to a breeding ranch. Up to now, he was a good bull. But like your great-grandpa always said, 'Never trust a bull.'"

Katy then piped up, "There's at least one good thing about all this, Ellie."

"What's that?"

"Now you have a bull story that's better than Crazy Uncle Steve's."

MONKEY MADNESS

Holding his bandaged right arm, Grady Cox slumped in a chair in the emergency room waiting area at the main hospital in Bangalore, India. Across from the 10-year-old American boy sat an Indian girl who was about his age. She was wearing a white blouse and dark gray skirt — a school uniform, he guessed — with a big dirt smudge on the front. She had a large gauze pad taped to her left leg.

"So what happened to you?" she asked.

"I got bitten by a monkey," replied Grady. "What about you?"

"The same bloody thing."

"Monkeys aren't very friendly around here, are they?"

"It's not just in Bangalore," she said. "It's happening everywhere throughout India, in big cities and small ones. I heard on the news that monkeys have been attacking hundreds of children at an old Hindu temple in Gauhati — that's in northeast India — over the past three weeks. The monkeys hide in trees and swoop down on kids and claw them and bite them."

"But why?" asked Grady.

"I'll tell you why," said an older Indian girl who had just checked into the emergency room and overheard their conversation. She was wearing a T-shirt and shorts splotched with bloodstains and had bandages on her right wrist and arm and left ear. "You're American?" she asked Grady. He nodded.

Not masking her bitterness, the teenager said, "My government has allowed the monkey population to get out of hand. We can't harm them because monkeys are a sacred symbol in Hinduism, and Hinduism is India's main religion. I'm a Hindu, and I love my religion, but I hate monkeys."

"Don't tell me you got attacked by a monkey, too," he said.

"Not just one," she replied. "A whole troop attacked me — in my house!"

Earlier that day, wherever Grady turned, he was experiencing something new — smelling incense made with sandalwood oil, seeing women in bold and colorful saris, hearing an old man play the sitar, tasting sugared peanuts from a vendor. Bangalore was all so different from his hometown in South Carolina.

Grady was in the bustling Indian city with his parents, who were on a business trip. They brought him along because they wanted him to see this exotic country. While his father was in a meeting, his mother took Grady for a walk to one of the city's ancient temples. On the way, a holy man presented Mrs. Cox with a flowered garland — a necklace of fresh marigolds strung together — which she put around her neck.

As he and his mother neared the temple, Grady had the feeling they were being watched. He looked up in the trees. "Hey, Mama, I see a monkey. Wait, I see another one...and another one. The trees are full of them!"

They were rhesus macaques, among the tens of thousands that have roamed freely in the cities of India for years. The stoutly built monkeys, which have silky brownish-yellow hair and distinctive reddish rumps, can weigh up to 20 pounds. They usually live in groups of 10 to 100, which are known as troops.

Grady didn't know that, over the years, India's rhesus monkeys had become increasingly aggressive, that they had been terrorizing and harassing people throughout the country. He didn't know that the monkeys were getting so bold they were even invading government offices in the capital of Delhi. He didn't know that the most dangerous monkeys were being "arrested" and sent to special "monkey prisons." So when a couple of monkeys were frolicking at his feet, Grady thought it was pretty cool.

One baby monkey took a liking to Mrs. Cox and ran up her leg, launched itself off her with a back flip, and scampered back to its mother. Then the baby did it again. "Why, isn't he just the cutest little thing you ever did see?" marveled Mrs. Cox. She asked Grady, "Sweetie pie, will you get a picture of this?"

He took off his backpack and fumbled around until he found his digital camera between a banana, an orange, bottled water, and a map. He pulled the camera out and took a shot as the little rhesus did its trick again. "I got it!" he exclaimed.

Then Grady moved closer to the monkeys that had gathered together near a bench and were grooming one another.

"Be careful," said his mother.

"They're just monkeys, Mama. They can't hurt us." He crouched down and grinned at them, his camera by his chest. "Hi, y'all. Look this way, please." He gave a wide, cheery smile.

Grady wasn't prepared for their reaction. In an

instant, five older monkeys swarmed on him so fast
and hard that he lost his balance and fell backward.
Screeching and snarling, the monkeys clawed at his bare
arms and legs. Grady got to his knees and tried to shake
the animals off him, but as soon as one fell, another
one jumped on him. "Get off!" he shrieked. "Get off!"

His mother tried to rescue him by swinging her purse
at them, shouting, "Shoo! Shoo! Go away!"

One of the monkeys sank its teeth into his right arm.
How can this be happening to me? Grady wondered.
Blood spurted down his arm. In desperation, he tried
flinging the rhesus off, but its jaws were locked on his
arm for several more seconds. *I can't believe this!*
Finally, with his left arm, Grady slugged the monkey in
the nose. Stunned by the blow, the rhesus let go and
scampered off.

An elderly man wearing a turban and carrying a small
doctor's bag hurried over to Grady. Without being
asked, the man wiped the bite wound with disinfectant
and placed a bandage over it. "Sadly, this happens too
often here," he said. "About two people a day are bitten
in this park, so I try to help." Turning to Mrs. Cox, he
said, "You wouldn't have a few rupees to help pay for
the cost of the first aid?" He held out his hand and
smiled. She reached into her purse and handed him five
dollars' worth of Indian money.

"Why did they attack me?" Grady whimpered. "I didn't do anything wrong."

"Unfortunately, you did," the man said. "When you smiled, you showed your teeth. To rhesus monkeys, showing teeth is a sign of hostility, so they attacked first. They didn't intend to bite you. But when you tried fighting them, one of them did."

Still shaking from the ordeal, Grady reached into his backpack for a bottle of water. "Hey, it's gone! So is all the fruit!" He looked on the ground and moaned. "And the camera, too! I had taken some great pictures."

"I'm sorry to say you probably won't ever see your camera again," the man said. "What they can't eat, they steal. They are bloody outrageous—and devious. Just the other day I saw a troop of monkeys steal food from a grocery stall. While one monkey bared its fangs and drove the terrified owner into a corner, the accomplices raided the fruit baskets at the front of the stall and made off with whatever they wanted."

Mrs. Cox hugged Grady and said, "You poor, poor dear. We need to get you to the hospital." She put her hand on her chest and looked down. "My garland! They took my garland!"

At that moment, she heard what sounded like high-pitched chatter coming from a banyan tree that grew behind the bench. On a branch above her was a rhesus scratching its belly and holding the stolen garland of marigolds. Making sure Mrs. Cox was watching, it casually plucked the orange flowers off the string necklace, and, one by one, popped them into its mouth.

About the same time, less than a mile away, 11-year-old Malkah Singh was riding her bicycle home from school. She kept her eyes peeled for the traffic, and also for the marauding rhesus troops that lived in the neighborhood. Random hit-and-run attacks on pedestrians and cyclists by monkeys weren't that uncommon, although she herself had never been a victim.

When it became increasingly harder to pedal, Malkah noticed that her rear tire was going flat. She had known for a week that it had a slow leak, but she had been too busy to get it fixed. However, she kept a manual bicycle pump in her book bag for just such an emergency.

She pulled over to the curb, laid her bike down, and removed her book bag. She got out the pump and began inflating the tire. Out of the corner of her eye, she saw her book bag move. She turned and saw that a rhesus had gripped the bag.

"Oh, no, you don't!" She dove to the ground and clutched one of the book bag's straps. The monkey wouldn't let go and tried to jerk it out of her hand.

Refusing to play tug-of-war with a monkey, Malkah held on to the book bag and stood up. Then she repeatedly twirled around until the rhesus, its feet now far off the ground, lost its grip and flew onto the sidewalk.

The monkey scurried down the street. "You better run, you bloody bad monkey!" Malkah shouted. She thought that was the last she would see of the rhesus.

Malkah knew instantly why the monkey wanted her book bag. Easily visible in a netted outside pocket were a banana left from lunch and a handful of toffee candy that a friend had given her. *That's what it was after, the little badmash,* she thought, using Indian slang for "naughty child."

After fixing the tire, Malkah continued on her way. Two blocks later at a stop sign, she waited for a truck to cross the intersection. She was straddling her bike when a blow to her back knocked her to the pavement. Catching her breath, she got up but felt a weight on her back. Looking behind her, she was startled to see the same monkey on her shoulders. It had ambushed her by dropping from a tree branch that was hanging over the street.

Now the screeching and chattering monkey was tearing at her book bag, which was still on her back. Wriggling and hopping in the middle of the street, Malkah swung her fists behind her head, trying to slug the monkey. She landed a lucky punch and knocked it off her shoulders. In retaliation, the rhesus bit her hard and deep in the calf of her left leg. Malkah howled in pain as the monkey scampered up the same tree it had leaped from.

When bystanders ran to help the girl, the monkey began pelting them with sticks. A policeman arrived, but there was little he could do. Because of monkeys' sacred status in Hinduism, he didn't dare shoot it no matter how ferocious it had become. He called for backup, hoping to catch the villain. But the rhesus jumped from treetop to treetop and easily fled the scene.

Only a few blocks away, 15-year-old Indira Pradesh, who was home alone with a fever, was awakened from her afternoon nap by clanging and scraping sounds and mewing coming from the kitchen. *What are those cats getting into?* she wondered.

Clad in shorts and a T-shirt, the barefoot girl padded toward the kitchen, ready to scold her pet kittens, Jadoo and Babu. When she entered the room, she screamed. Three large rhesus monkeys had cornered the terrified kittens and were pulling on their ears and tails like tormenting bullies.

Waving her arms, Indira yelled, "Scoot! Scoot!" The monkeys began hooting and jumped up onto the counter where an overturned fruit bowl lay amid peels of bananas and oranges that the intruders had already eaten. "How did you get in here?"

The windows were open, but they had bars installed specifically to keep the monkeys out. Then she discovered that the back door was wide open. She knew she had closed it before taking her nap, although she hadn't locked it. "You opened the *door*?" she said in disbelief to the three monkeys.

Looking out through the open door, she saw two more monkeys in her mother's garden. They were pulling out the roots and bulbs of her ornamentals, scattering the petals and trampling the neat rows of what once had been a picture-perfect garden. "Oh, no! Not Mother's flowers!" She hurried outside to chase them away.

Then two more monkeys leaped down from a backyard tree and swung on a 20-foot-high utility wire until it snapped. They plunged into a rosebush and smashed it.

Indira dashed back into the house. The monkeys—she counted at least six inside now—were ransacking the kitchen. They had already scattered bowls, pots, and pans on the counters. They had opened the refrigerator and were flinging containers of food onto the floor where they splattered open, creating a gooey mess.

They squished raw eggs with their hands and stuffed fruits and vegetables into their mouths.

Overwhelmed, Indira reached for the phone to call for help. But the line was dead. *They broke the telephone wire!* she told herself. *I can't leave or they'll trash the entire house. I'll have to fight them on my own.*

Indira turned on the radio and raised the volume to full blast, hoping it would drive them away, but they ignored it. So she grabbed a broom and began swinging it at them. "Get out of here! Get out of here right now!"

Three of the rhesus scurried out the back door, so she turned her attention to the others that were at the opposite end of the kitchen. As she advanced toward them with her broom, they screamed and leaped over her head. While flying through the air, one of them knocked the broom out of Indira's hands. She spun around and chased them out of the house, but then she froze. Standing in the doorway alone was the largest rhesus she had ever seen — and it looked mean.

It hissed, flashed its teeth, and moved toward Indira. Unarmed and unsure of what to do, Indira stood completely still. Again the monkey pulled back its lips, showing a line of horrible yellow fangs.

Do something! Before she could react, the rhesus leaped on her chest. Indira staggered back while trying to push it off of her, but the monkey was too quick. It bit her on the upper right arm and then went after her face. She grabbed the rhesus around the throat and moved her head away from its teeth. Still, it managed to rip a piece of her left ear. Indira tried to strangle the attacker but she was too weak from her fever, so she ran forward and slammed the monkey against the pantry door. The rhesus let out a shriek and then bit her right wrist before jumping off the girl and fleeing outside.

Within seconds, all the monkeys had vanished.

"It's almost like the monkeys are trying to take over the whole country," Grady said to Indira and Malkah after the three of them had traded stories of their attacks while they waited with their families in the emergency room.

"It seems that way," said Indira. "Part of the problem is that our population is growing and we're taking over land where the monkeys live. They're forced to move and search for new sources of food and water, so they come into the city and raid garbage bins, stores, buildings, and homes like mine."

"And they attack people like me," said Malkah.

"And they steal food and cameras from tourists like me," Grady added.

"Unfortunately, there is little the government can or will do," said Indira. "As the monkey population in the cities grows, the situation will only get worse. The hospitals see monkey-attack victims like us every day."

Grady asked, "So what will the doctors do to us here?"

"You're not afraid of needles, are you?" Indira replied.

Minutes later, the emergency room staff treated the bite wounds of Grady, Malkah, and Indira. The three young people were given the first of a series of five shots of rabies vaccine for added protection.

For the rest of the semester, Malkah refused to take her bicycle to school. Instead, she walked with a group of friends, believing there was safety in numbers. She also carried a walking stick, which doubled as a weapon in case any rhesus dared try to assault her. Fortunately, she never had to use it.

After the attack, Indira and her family made sure the doors to their house remained locked even when they were home during the day. They didn't want those clever monkeys sneaking inside by turning the door handles. But the pesky animals still harassed the family every now and then.

They would snatch clothes that had been hanging out in the backyard to dry and carry them high into the trees and leave them there. More than once, Indira had to climb a tree to retrieve a shirt or underwear that had been left dangling from a branch.

Once, she found a baby rhesus playing in a just-washed towel that was drying outside. The little monkey wrapped itself up in the towel and rolled around while its mother looked on in amusement. Indira didn't find it funny, but she left them alone. She knew better than to get into another fight with a rhesus.

After Grady returned home to South Carolina, he realized that despite his terrible ordeal, he was glad he had visited India because it was such a fascinating country. Besides, he came away with at least one exciting experience to tell his friends. It was a shame, though, that he didn't have any pictures to show them.

THE BREAKING
POINT

"Jessie! Get away from the ice!" ordered Robby Hackett. "You'd think you would've learned your lesson after the last time we were out here."

The yellow Labrador retriever skidded to a stop just as she was about to spring onto a frozen creek. She looked over at her 10-year-old master and whined as if she were pleading with him for permission to run across the creek and continue chasing a rabbit. But Jessie was an obedient two-year-old, so after a couple of barks at the rabbit she turned around and bounded in the snow to Robby. "Good girl, Jessie," he said, pounding her back with his gloved hands. "Thanks for listening to me."

Two weeks earlier, Jessie had wandered onto a frozen pond only to have the ice crack and buckle under her. She slipped into the frigid water and yelped for help.

Fortunately, she was near the edge of the pond, so Robby was able to reach out from the bank and yank her to safety.

Now the freckle-faced boy and his canine pal were trudging in fresh, foot-deep snow in the woods behind their home in northern Maine. They were on their way to meet his fourth-grade classmates Tony Angelli and Max Schultz at a clearing about a half mile away where they planned to build a snow fort.

Robby drew the parka hood tighter over his red hair to ward off the chill from a breeze that made the 30-degree temperature feel more like 20. At least the sun was shining, making the snow dust glisten as it flew in front of his sunglasses. The snow on the boughs of the swaying pine trees reminded Robby of vanilla icing on Christmas-tree cookies. He loved winter days like this.

When he neared the clearing, he didn't see the boys, but he did spot two sets of fresh footprints in the snow that split up. One headed to a tree in front of him on the left and the other to a tree on the right. Jessie began wagging her tail.

"Wait a second," said Robby warily. "I think we're walking into an ambush, Jess—"

Thwack! Thwack! Two snowballs splattered onto the front of his bright red ski jacket and two more struck his legs before he dove for cover behind a large rock.

Thinking that the surprise attack was great fun, Jessie kept twirling around and barking, trying to catch flying snowballs with her mouth. After quickly forming four snowballs and cradling them in his right arm, the left-handed Robby rushed out from behind his cover. In rapid-fire fashion, he nailed Tony, who had been hiding behind a fir tree. When he was out of ammo, Robby charged after Max, who threw a flurry of snowballs. Robby ducked and bobbed out of the way and tackled his much smaller friend. Then Robby scooped up a handful of snow and rubbed it in Max's face.

"We're even now," he declared, flashing a triumphant grin. He extended his hand to Max and pulled him to his feet. Tony came out of hiding and the three of them agreed to a truce. It was time to build their fort.

They decided to locate it within range of the path because it was a popular trail for cross-country skiers like Robby's 15-year-old brother, Kevin. Robby was hoping to bombard Kevin and Kevin's friend Will Harris in retaliation for them stuffing handfuls of snow down his back earlier that morning.

Robby, Max, and Tony rolled large, dense snowballs and placed them side by side for their fort's four-sided foundation. They packed the snow and filled up each crack and crevice, forming four solid, chest-high walls, and they left a small exit in the back.

While they began molding dozens of snowballs in preparation for the "enemy" to ski past them, Jessie began growling. "What is it, girl?" Robby asked.

Tony stuck his head above the wall and said, "Hey, guys—look!" He pointed at a bull moose that appeared on the trail 50 feet away from them. The animal, which had already shed his winter antlers, was a large adult.

It wasn't uncommon for the boys to see a moose. Outside of Alaska, Maine has the largest population of moose in the United States, and northern Maine is considered prime moose country. As the largest members of the deer family, moose can weigh more than a thousand pounds and stand more than seven feet tall. In summer they eat leaves and wetland plants to build up their weight in fat for the winter when food becomes scarce. Moose tend to travel alone, although a cow moose might have one or two calves with her. Because their main predators are wolves and bears, moose usually aren't afraid of humans. As a result, they go wherever they want—including into the middle of towns and even people's backyards. These huge animals seldom hurry; they simply go about their business, often acting as though the people watching them aren't even there.

Moose normally aren't aggressive, but they are big and unpredictable, and on rare occasions they have been known to stomp on people for no apparent reason. In some cases, a cow moose will attack a person who is between her and her calf. Moose that have been fed by people — which is illegal — can also be dangerous.

Although they have long, gangly legs, homely faces, and ungainly bodies, Robby felt there was something majestic about moose, and he always enjoyed watching them. Jessie, on the other hand, acted as though moose were an embarrassment to the animal kingdom and must be harassed at every opportunity.

Inside the snow fort, Jessie was running back and forth, howling and woofing, wanting to dash out and drive the moose from the area. Robby ordered her to keep quiet and heel, which she did reluctantly.

As he gazed at the moose, which was now strolling along the trail closer to the boys, Tony and Max jumped up and hurled snowballs at the animal. All but one struck the moose on his shoulder and flank, causing him to hurry his pace and veer off into the woods.

"What did you do that for?" Robby snapped.

"Because the moose is ugly," Tony replied.

"Well, he's not as ugly as you."

Tony fired a snowball that struck Robby in the chest.

"They're goofy-looking," said Max. "It's like if you cut up pictures of different animals and then took some of the pieces to make a new one, you'd come up with a moose. You got to admit, they are butt ugly."

Robby frowned. "But, man, it's not right to mess with a moose."

"Maybe not, but it sure is fun," said Tony.

"Shush," ordered Max in a quiet voice. "They're coming! Get down! And keep your dog quiet, Robby."

Skiing on the trail were Kevin and his friend Will, who paid little attention to the snow fort.

"Wait," whispered Tony to Max and Robby. "Wait... Wait... Now!"

The boys jumped up from behind the wall of their fort and fired round after round at the two teenage skiers. Kevin and Will skied off the trail until they were out of range. They took off their skis and stormed the fort, swinging their ski poles like baseball bats to break up the flying snowballs. When Kevin and Will reached the fort, they kicked down the walls and squashed the remaining pile of snowballs. Jessie was jumping up and down, wagging her tail, and barking at all the excitement. She wasn't sure what to do because, as the family dog, she was just as loyal to Kevin as she was to Robby.

Once the fort was destroyed, the teens hustled back to their skis, clipped them on, and continued on their way.

After surveying the smashed walls, Tony announced, "I've had all the fun I can stand. You guys want to come over to my house? I got a new basketball video game."

"Sure," replied Max. "What about you, Robby?"

Robby shook his head. "Thanks, but Jessie and I are going home." He and his dog then headed off in the opposite direction.

At a point where the trail narrowed and curved through a stand of thick hemlock and brush, Jessie stopped and smelled around a tree trunk. Her ears perked up, her eyes opened wide, and her tail started wagging. She had latched onto a scent that she simply had to follow.

With her nose to the ground, she headed deeper into the woods. "Jessie, get back here!" ordered Robby. But Jessie was so keen on tracking the scent that she ignored him and slipped into a thicket and disappeared. "Jessie!" he shouted.

Suddenly, the dog began baying like a hound. *She must have treed a raccoon,* Robby thought. *I better go get her.* He marched into the heavy brush, and as he shoved away low-hanging branches, clumps of snow fell on him, making it even harder to see. Jessie's yowling was getting louder and had reached a higher pitch. Robby wasn't sure, but he thought he heard snorting.

Just then, Jessie came rushing from the thicket and, with her tail between her legs, raced past Robby. *I've got a bad feeling about this,* he told himself. Before another thought could enter the boy's mind, the moose that he had seen earlier burst through the brush. The animal wasn't friendly.

His head swept back and forth and his hooves landed from side to side as he ran after the dog. Robby, directly in front of the moose's path, froze. He wanted to dive out of the way, but he couldn't because the thick brush made it nearly impossible to move. *Oh, no. I'm going to get stomped!* He leaned against the brush, crouched, covered his face, and waited for the impact. The moose roared by, missing him by inches and leaving behind a strong, musty odor that made Robby gag.

He turned his head and saw the moose and Jessie jockeying for position to attack each other in a small clearing. The dog barked and bayed, dodging this way and that, while the moose pawed the ground and snorted. The moose lowered his head and, swinging it from side to side, tried to ram Jessie, but the dog nimbly managed to weave her way around and between the animal's long legs.

With the moose determined to crush the dog, Robby untangled himself from the brush and tried to climb a small juniper. But the branch that held his weight snapped and he plunged to the snowy ground.

The moose then turned his attention to Robby. They stared at each other. *Uh-oh. This doesn't look good,*

Robby told himself. His heart was beating so hard that he could hear it under the hood of his jacket. *There's no place for me to escape.* The moose lowered his head, white clouds of steam jetting from his flared nostrils. The long hairs on his hump bristled straight up, his ears lay flat, and he licked his lips — classic signs that he was about to make another charge, only this time at Robby.

However, Jessie lunged once again at the moose, barking fiercely until the animal forgot about Robby and focused again on flattening the dog. "Jessie! Get away from that moose! Jessie!" The dog darted in and out, left and right, barely avoiding the stomping hooves. Soon Jessie spun around and scampered toward Robby, who was hiding behind a wide oak tree.

When the dog joined him, Robby stepped out and waved his arms and hollered, hoping he could scare the angry moose. He stopped about 10 feet from him and glared with furious eyes at him. Robby knew enough about moose to know that, in tense showdowns between man and beast, the best course of action is often to be patient, that after a stare-down, the moose may lose interest and walk away. He kept a hand on Jessie's head, trying to keep her calm. He could feel her shivering. "Calm down," he said softly to his dog. But the words were meant for himself as well. After a

standoff that lasted about 10 minutes, the moose
finally retreated and disappeared into the woods as if
nothing had happened.

"Whew, that was close," Robby told Jessie. "He was
one mean moose. He's grumpy probably because he's
hungry. That big snowfall we had last week could have
made it hard for him to find food. Well, at least the
worst is over with."

If only that had been true.

They returned to the trail and, not seeing any moose
tracks in the snow, slogged their way toward home at a
fast clip. But then Robby heard a tromping sound
coming from the tree line. He looked back to see the
looming silhouette of the same moose, ears back and
hair up, galloping toward him in a dead run.

No! Not again! Why is he after me? It took about
three precious seconds before Robby could get his feet
in gear. *If I can just make it to those trees and climb up
one of them, maybe I'll be safe.* "Jessie! Run! Run!"

But Jessie kept her ground. Robby scurried to a maple
tree and began climbing it when he heard Jessie let out
a frantic, high-pitched yelp. *She's been hurt!* Like most
moose, when this one charged, he kicked forward with
his front hooves. One of his hooves landed on Jessie's
right front leg. The dog whined in pain and, half
limping, half scooting, tried to escape from the moose,

but the huge animal caught up with her and rammed her, sending Jessie rolling in the snow.

He's going to stomp her to death! I've got to do something!

Jumping down from the tree, Robby shouted, "Noooo!" Blinded by love for his dog, Robby forgot about his own safety. He raced over to Jessie, screaming and waving his arms like a crazed chimpanzee, hoping to stop the moose from killing his dog. It seemed to work. The moose backed off far enough away so that Robby could reach the whimpering dog, who was lying on her side. "Please, girl, get up," he urged. "Come on, you can do it." With some effort, Jessie got up and, holding her injured paw in the air, hobbled on three legs toward the trees.

When they reached the tree line, Robby looked over his shoulder. The moose had his back turned to him. *Thank goodness. Now maybe he'll go away and leave us alone.*

Robby bent down and examined his injured dog, now resting on her belly in the snow. "How bad are you hurt, girl?" He felt over her body, looking for injuries. Her nose was bleeding and swelling up from a kick to the head, and her front leg was definitely broken. When he pressed gently on her right side, she whined in pain. *I wonder if her ribs are broken.*

His train of thought was broken by that tromping sound again. He wheeled around just in time to see the moose galloping right for them. The beast was so close that Robby knew he didn't have time to get up and run, so he made himself into a ball, fearing the worst. He screamed in agony when a hoof crashed down on his ankle. Another hoof brushed by his head, and a third grazed his back. He tightened into a smaller ball, covering his head with his arms.

This can't be happening to me! He's going to kill me! The moose kicked him in the rear, sending a sharp pain zipping up his back and leaving him gasping for breath. The irate moose then purposely walked back and forth over Robby as though he were dribbling with a soccer ball instead of a frightened, helpless boy.

During this latest attack, Jessie couldn't stand to see her master in trouble. She stood up on only three legs and tried to defend him. Barking and yelping, she nipped at the moose until it stopped trampling Robby. Jessie kept backing up, drawing the animal away from her wounded master.

Peeking out from under his arms, Robby saw the brave, limping dog harass the moose. *Now's my chance to escape,* he thought. He tried to stand up, but his ankle hurt too much, so he crawled through the snow until he reached the trunk of a fallen tree. He waited and watched, praying that the moose wouldn't kill his dog. Jessie proved to be a worthy opponent. The moose finally had enough and walked off.

"Jessie, come here!" The dog limped over to him and lay down next to Robby. Hugging her around the neck, he said, "You're the bravest dog in the whole world. Thanks for saving my life."

He couldn't tell if he was bleeding, because he was all bundled up. Fortunately, his four layers of clothes — long-sleeved T-shirt, flannel shirt, heavy wool sweater, and ski jacket — helped protect his body from the hooves. His hooded jacket was tattered, and his gloves and sunglasses were lost during the attack. Although every part of his body was sore, he knew things could have been much worse.

"At least we're both alive, huh, Jessie?" Robby's ankle was throbbing. He shoved snow into his hiking boot, hoping it would help ease the pain and swelling, but he couldn't put any weight on it. "My ankle, it's broken," he told his dog. "Jessie, we're not far from home. Go home. If Mom sees you, she'll come look for me."

Jessie whimpered. She understood the command, but she refused to leave her master. "Okay, okay, I guess that was unfair," Robby told her. "It's hard for you to walk, too. We'll try going together." Crawling in the snow, Robby found a large dead branch below an oak tree and used it as a crutch.

Which way should we go? he wondered. *If we take the trail, we might run into the moose again...and the next time we might not be so lucky. He could kill us. If we go the long way through the forest, we won't make it home until after dark...and I'm not sure Jessie or I can walk that far because we're hurt.* "Jessie, let's take the trail."

Constantly on guard for signs of the moose, Robby and his dog slowly and painfully hobbled toward home. An hour later, as the sun dipped below the treetops, Robby looked up and smiled. A few hundred yards away, he could see smoke wafting out of the chimney of his house. "Jessie, we're going to make it!"

But then...*thump, thump, thump!* "Oh, no!" Instinctively, Robby dove for the ground, crunched up in a ball, and covered his head. *Not the moose again!* He heard Jessie barking excitedly, only it wasn't a frantic yelp. It was her happy bark, the one she gave when Robby and Kevin came home from school.

"Why are you all curled up?"

Robby lifted his head, opened his eyes, and looked up. It was Kevin. "Our snowballs couldn't have hurt you that much."

What Robby had thought was the start of another moose attack had been Kevin and Will plastering him with snowballs after returning from their cross-country skiing excursion. They were laughing at Robby until they realized he and Jessie were hurt. After hearing about his little brother's ordeal, Kevin carried Robby on his back the rest of the way home while Will brought Jessie.

The battered boy was taken to the hospital, where he was treated for a broken ankle and bruised ribs. The dog was driven to the animal clinic, where she was treated for a broken leg.

Later that night, the whole family gathered in front of the fireplace. Robby and Jessie lay on the floor, each with their injured limb in a cast.

"I just got off the phone with a wildlife officer," Robby's father said. "He told me this moose got aggressive because he was hungry and tired of walking in deep snow. To make matters worse, he got harassed by Jessie and by your friends who threw snowballs at him. Each moose has a different breaking point, and apparently the one you met today had reached his."

Pointing to the cast on his ankle and to the one on Jessie's leg, Robby added, "And we reached our breaking points, too — but ours hurt a whole lot more than the moose's."

THE STALKER

Jake Minot was a smart sixth-grader, but lately he had been distracted at school. He couldn't help it because his grandfather, Sam Youngblood, whom he adored, was undergoing treatment for a serious lung problem.

Sampa — the name Jake had given his grandfather when the boy was old enough to talk — was a burly, bearded outdoorsman who grew up in the wilds of British Columbia. For years, he made his living as a guide for vacationing hunters and fishermen. He also had a contract with the Ministry of Environment to track down and capture or kill dangerous animals that had attacked livestock or people. But because of his illness, he had to retire.

As he did at least twice a week after school, Jake had the bus driver drop him off at Sampa's log cabin, which was located on a gravel road that led to Jake's house a half mile away. Now that Sampa was ill, it troubled Jake to see his once brawny, broad-shouldered grandfather losing weight and coughing all the time. At least Sampa still had his thatch of curly gray-brown hair and bushy eyebrows.

Jake knocked on the door and entered without waiting for a response. His grandfather had been sleeping in his easy chair, a book on his lap. He woke up with a start and then broke out in a wide grin. "Jakey!" he said with a wheeze.

"How are you feeling today, Sampa?"

His grandfather, whose flannel shirt and jeans seemed two sizes too big for him, coughed twice before replying, "Doing great, Jakey, just great." It was the same answer Sampa always gave, whether he was feeling well or not. But each day, his voice seemed a little weaker and raspier and his coughing jags seemed to last a little longer.

The stocky, muscular boy took off his Calgary Flames cap and ran his fingers through his unruly, ear-covering black hair. "What a day at school," he said. "I forgot I had to give an oral book report on *The Call of the Wild* today, and I didn't have my notes, but I fumbled through it." He slipped off his book bag and asked, "So what's new?"

"Something interesting happened yesterday," Sampa

said. "A friend of mine, Ray Stuckey, has some sheep penned behind a five-foot-tall galvanized fence. Well, don't you know, the night before last a cougar got in there, killed a full-grown sheep, and took it over the fence and dragged it about two hundred yards to the base of a huge red cedar tree. The tree was rotted out on one side, and there the cougar had made what we call its layup — not a lair, but a place where it rests after the kill. A cougar can get exhausted taking down a kill because it's really hard work.

"This morning, Ray picked me up and took me out to look at that layup, and don't you know I found tracks of a female cougar and her kitten. They had devoured that sheep, and there was nothing left but a few bones and a cracked skull. But the funniest thing was the wool they'd left behind. The cougar has an abrasive tongue and uses it to break off the hair from a kill by licking it. The mother and kitten had stacked up the hair by the carcass before they ate the sheep. Those cougars are the neatest creatures. Not like me."

Pointing to a picture of his late wife, who had died three years earlier, Sampa said, "Oh, how your grandma would get on my case for being so messy. Every day I'd bring home a rabbit or a half-dozen quail or some walleyes to clean and gut and I'd make a mess. And she'd say, 'Sam, for crying out loud, this is a house, not a butcher shop.' Every day. We were married for forty-five years, so how many times would that be? You're smart, Jakey. You can do the math."

"Math?" The word triggered a sinking feeling in Jake — a realization that he had once again forgotten some schoolwork. "Uh-oh." He dug through his book bag and groaned. "Oh, great. I left my math book in my locker, and my homework assignment is due tomorrow. Mom and Dad will kill me. They said if I missed any more homework assignments I wouldn't be able to go fishing the rest of this semester."

"Ouch. That's pretty severe, Jakey. Do you want me to drive you to school?"

"It's ten miles away. By the time we get there, the doors will be locked. Besides, you're not supposed to be driving. But I've got an idea."

Jake phoned his classmate Tim Murphy, who lived in the forest two miles from Sampa's house and about a mile from Jake's. Out of earshot of his grandfather, Jake explained his dilemma to Tim. "I'll hike over to your house, get the math book, and hurry home before my parents get off work. I can do it all in under an hour. I know I'm not supposed to hike solo, but this is an emergency."

"Yeah, no fishing for three months," said Tim. "That's harsh for missing a homework assignment."

After he hung up the phone, Jake went into the living room and said, "Sampa, I've got to go now." He slung his book bag over his Flames sweatshirt, gave his grandfather a hug, and hurried out the door before Sampa could ask any questions.

Jake hustled along a trail that took him through an area dotted with large boulders and shaded by tall pine trees. Ten minutes into his trek, he followed a bend in the path and halted. About 100 feet in front of him was a magnificent cougar sprawled on its belly across the trail, gnawing on a stick.

Jake had never seen a cougar in the wild. He admired its sleek, muscular beauty and its yellowish-brown fur. From the end of its long black-tipped tail to its pink nose, it was about eight feet in length. The big cat lifted its broad head, revealing whitish fur on its throat and chest and blackish stripes on its muzzle and behind its ears. It sniffed the air and then slowly rose and ambled off into the trees, its sharp, curved claws clicking on the stony path.

"Oh, wow," Jake murmured in awe. He tingled with excitement, knowing that he had encountered a wild animal that most people have never seen. But once the animal disappeared into the woods, Jake felt a little spooked. He remembered what Sampa had once told him: *The cougar is the most unpredictable animal I've*

*ever run into, very difficult to track, the kind of animal
that will change its direction—just turn right around—
for no apparent reason. It's a secretive, sleek, and
sneaky creature, the shyest wild animal in North
America. Give it one leaf and it'll hide behind it, hide
itself as no other animal can do.*

Jake's legs began to shake. He knew cougars are
fierce solitary hunters with excellent eyesight and
superb hearing; that they feed primarily on white-tailed
deer but will also eat smaller game such as opossums,
rabbits, and mice; that they run swiftly and silently,
climb trees and boulders with ease, and even swim.

He also knew that rather than simply chasing after
their food, cougars prefer stalking their prey at close
range, utilizing the element of surprise. At the last
moment, a cougar might leap as far as 20 feet or more
onto the back of its victim. Strong jaws and long teeth
make it possible for cougars to kill their prey with one
bite on the nape of the neck. Jake shuddered when he
thought about yet another cougar habit: After it kills its
victim and eats some of it, a cougar often covers the
remains with leaves or other debris to be saved for a
later meal.

His mouth now suddenly drained of all saliva by the
uneasiness that had crept over him, Jake pulled out
the Swiss Army knife that he always kept in his pocket

and opened its two-inch blade. *A lot of good this will do me,* he thought. *But it's better than nothing.*

He had a decision to make. *Should I go on or turn around? I really need that book. I'm only about fifteen minutes away from Tim's house. I think I'll wait a little while and let the cougar move on and then I'll keep going.*

About five minutes later, Jake started walking cautiously, paying close attention to any sounds around him. After about a hundred yards, he gulped and muttered, "Oh, no." Up ahead was the cougar again, crouched in some bushes, watching him.

I've got to go back, he told himself. *Forget about the math book. I'm better off facing Mom and Dad's anger than getting eaten by a cougar.*

Jake had been taught never to turn his back on a dangerous animal, so he began to backpedal while focusing on the big cat's piercing gray-brown eyes. He was somewhat encouraged that it didn't make any aggressive moves. *Don't go too fast and you'll be okay,* he told himself. Within a minute, he rounded a curve in the trail and was out of the animal's sight. Then he turned toward Sampa's house and quickened his pace. Jake was beginning to feel a little safer, but just as his comfort level rose, so did his pulse because the cougar abruptly appeared about 30 yards in front of him.

While keeping its eyes locked on Jake's, the big cat lowered its head and started walking toward him.

I'm in trouble now. Jake gripped his Swiss Army knife in his right hand and quickly considered his options. *I can't outrun it. There's no place to hide. There's only one thing to do.*

Jake yelled at the top of his lungs, jumped up and down, and raised his arms to make himself look bigger and as menacing as possible. His actions caused the cougar to stop about 10 yards from him. The big cat tweaked its head and eyed him curiously as if wondering what sort of creature was making such a ruckus. To Jake's relief, the cougar turned away, jumped onto a boulder on the side of the path, stretched out, and then began to lick its thick paws. Every few seconds, it glanced at Jake.

Maybe it has lost interest in me, Jake thought. *Or maybe it's just toying with me.*

Keeping his eyes on the cougar as much as possible, Jake stole quick glimpses around his feet. Slowly, he bent down and picked up a rock that weighed about four pounds. With his knife in one hand and a rock in his other hand, Jake once again backed up, only this time in the opposite direction, toward Tim's house.

Jake had covered about 50 yards when, to his dismay, the cougar blocked his way once more. *Oh, great. It's boxing me in. It's definitely toying with me. That's not a good sign.*

The cougar glared at him and slowly began advancing until it was so close that Jake could smell the animal's musky, sweaty odor. It began to growl and bare its teeth.

Jake felt his legs about to buckle from fear. Pumped by terror, streams of sweat rolled down his arms into his hands, making it hard to keep a grip on the knife and rock.

For the second time, Jake jumped up and down, waved his arms, and shouted, "Get outta here! Go! Go! Go!"

His faced turned pale because instead of retreating as he had hoped, the cougar showed absolutely no fear and moved directly in front of him. The cougar glowered, its ears up and alert. Jake backed up and kept yelling, but the cougar advanced anyway. The big cat squinted, flared its nostrils, and flattened its ears.

For Jake there was nowhere to run, nowhere to hide.

With a frightening growl, the cougar leaped and crashed into Jake's chest, knocking him off the trail and down an embankment. Before Jake had stopped rolling, the cougar was on top of him, clawing and biting his chest and neck. Amazingly, Jake had held onto the rock and knife. He bashed the rock against the animal's head, temporarily stunning it just enough for Jake to wriggle free and jump up.

The cougar backed away for a few seconds and then stopped to lick blood off its claws — Jake's blood.

Breathing heavily, Jake slowly walked backward until he was out of sight of the animal. Then he began running toward Sampa's house. But as soon as he reached a switchback, he spotted the cougar again, this time on top of a boulder next to the trail. The animal was trying to get into position for another attack. *It's stalking me!*

Before Jake could react, the cougar leaped at him again, but Jake ducked, and it flew over his crouched body. As the big cat whirled around for another assault, Jake flung the rock, bouncing it off the animal's head. The cougar let out a yowl and backed off, giving Jake a few precious seconds to whip off his backpack and start swinging it at the big cat.

The cougar stayed just out of range. Keeping it at bay, Jake walked backward down the trail, but the animal refused to let him escape.

The big cat charged, leaped, and tore into Jake. When they both hit the ground, everything turned dark and smelly for Jake. His head was now in the cougar's mouth, and the cat's teeth were digging into the top of his skull. Searching for a firmer hold, it relaxed its jaws for a second and then bit Jake's head a second time, sinking its sharp feline teeth deep into the muscles of his neck. It shook its head just as if it was shaking the life out of a rabbit. The attack was carried out in dead silence. There was no growling, no hissing, no snarling.

The only noise came from Jake. But his screams and grunts were muted because his head was still in the cougar's mouth.

It's going to kill you! he thought. *Fight! Fight with everything you've got!*

Blood trickled over his face and into his ears. Still gripping his knife, Jake slashed at the cougar's throat, but because of its thick fur and skin, Jake failed to draw blood. Raising the knife high over the animal's head, he twice plunged it into the back of its neck, but the big cat didn't even whimper.

Only then did Jake realize that the knife's blade had closed on his index finger. Reaching over the cougar's head with his other hand, he managed to pry the knife open. Then with all the force he could muster, he thrust the knife into the big cat's skull with his right hand while jabbing his left thumb into its right eye. The cougar shrieked. It released its hold on his head, pulled its claws from his neck, and jumped backward.

From his knees, Jake hurled another rock that struck the cougar's side. He stood up, wiped the blood off his face, and backed his way down the trail. When he could no longer see the animal, he ran toward Sampa's house. Jake didn't know how badly he was hurt, but he figured it was serious based on the amount of blood that streamed down his face and neck.

About five minutes from the house, he glanced over his shoulder. *No! It can't be!* But it was. The cougar had just hopped onto a boulder behind him, its eyes trained directly at him. *Don't stop now. Keep going. Why won't it leave me alone?*

Fully panicked, Jake raced down the trail, wondering if or when the big cat would attack him for the third time. Every few seconds, he looked back. Sometimes he saw the animal stalking him, other times he didn't see it at all. He reached a clearing. *Now I'm only three minutes away from Sampa's....* He rock-hopped across a stream. *Two more minutes...*

From out of nowhere, the cougar leaped onto Jake's back. Turning over on his back, Jake clutched the cat by the neck, but the animal was much too powerful for him. It came in for the kill, its teeth ready to rip out Jake's throat, when three gunshots rang out.

The cougar froze, let out a whimpering yowl, and then fell limp on top of Jake. He squirmed out from under the dead animal and looked up. "Sampa!" Standing over him was his grandfather, clutching his trusty rifle.

Sampa didn't say a word. He whipped off his flannel shirt and wrapped it around Jake's bleeding head, which had been shredded by the cougar's claws and teeth.

As he helped his grandson into the house, Sampa said, "When you left, I looked out the window and saw that you didn't take the road to your house. You took the path in the woods. I figured you were headed to your friend Tim's house, so I started following you to make sure you'd be all right, but you were moving too fast for me. I thought while I was out here with my rifle, I'd do a little rabbit hunting. Then I came upon you and the cougar. Jakey, I'm so thankful you're alive."

Although he wasn't supposed to drive, Sampa took Jake to the hospital, where the boy needed more than 70 stitches to close up the wounds to his head, neck, and hands. The next day Sampa showed up in Jake's hospital room.

"I went back and examined the cougar," Sampa reported. "Now I know why he attacked you. He was starving. There was nothing in his stomach but water, and porcupine quills were in his throat. Those stickers were his last meal, and they hurt him. He was in pain."

"I'm so sorry, Sampa. I should never have gone out there alone and without a weapon. Now I'm laid up in the hospital and my head has more stitches than a soccer ball. And a cougar is dead."

"Yeah, well, you have even bigger problems."

"I do?"

With a wink and a smile, Sampa said, "You failed to turn in your math homework."